Glen Canyon

Glen Canyon

An Archaeological Summary

Jesse D. Jennings

Foreword by Don D. Fowler

THE UNIVERSITY OF UTAH PRESS

SALT LAKE CITY, UTAH

Originally published by
The University of Utah Press as
Glen Canyon: A Summary
University of Utah Anthropological Paper 81
(Glen Canyon Series 31) 1966.

LIBRARY OF CONGRESS CATALOGING-IN-PUBLICATION DATA

Jennings, Jesse David, 1909–
    Glen Canyon : an archaeological summary / Jesse D. Jennings ;
foreword by Don D. Fowler.
            p.   cm.
    Originally published: 1966, in series: Anthropological papers /
University of Utah, Dept. of Anthropology ; no. 81. Glen Canyon
series ; no. 31.
    Includes bibliographical references.
    ISBN 0-87480-584-8 (alk. paper)
    1. Indians of North America—Utah—Antiquities. 2. Indians of
North America—Glen Canyon (Utah and Ariz.)—Antiquities.
3. Salvage archaeology—Glen Canyon (Utah and Ariz.) 4. Glen
Canyon (Utah and Ariz.)—Antiquities. I. Title.
E78.U55J459 1998   98-18981
979.2'59—dc21

Contents

Illustrations

Foreword

Don D. Fowler

In the published version of his diary of his epochal trip through the
canyons of the Colorado River in 1869, John Wesley Powell wrote,

> The features of this canyon are greatly diversified. . . . [There are] verti-
> cal walls at times. These are usually found to stand above great curves.
> The river, sweeping around these bends, undermines the cliffs in places.
> Sometimes the rocks are overhanging; in other curves, curious, narrow
> glens are found. Through these we climb . . . to where a spring bursts
> out from under an overhanging cliff, and where cottonwoods and wil-
> lows stand, while, along the curves of the brooklet, oaks grow, and
> other rich vegetation is seen, in marked contrast to the general appear-
> ance of naked rock. We call these Oak Glens. . . .
>
> On the walls, and back many miles into the country, numbers of
> monument-shaped buttes are observed. So we have a curious *ensemble*
> of wonderful features—carved walls, royal arches, glens, alcove
> gulches, mounds and monuments. From which of these features shall
> we select a name? We decide to call it Glen Canyon (1969: 96–97).

Glen Canyon! For nearly a century, the name and the place were
mysterious, fabled. After Powell's trips of 1869 and 1871–72, probably
less than three hundred people ever "ran the river," boated through the
canyons of the Colorado, and especially Glen Canyon—until the mid-
1950s when final plans were announced to build the Glen Canyon Dam
and create Lake Powell behind it. Now more people visit the Lake Powell National Recreation Area annually than any other unit of the National Park Service, including Yellowstone and Yosemite.

The dam and the lake were controversial in the 1950s, and still are
four decades later and counting (see Martin, 1989). For example, on
March 13, 1963, the long-time Executive Director of the Sierra Club—
a man the writer John McFee (1971) called the "Arch Druid" for his
life-long efforts to preserve and protect the sublimity of the natural
world—David Brower, wrote,

Glen Canyon died in 1963 and I was partly responsible for its needless death. So were you. Neither you nor I, nor anyone else, knew it well enough to insist that at all costs it should endure. When we began to find out, it was too late. On January 21, 1963, the last day on which the execution of one of the planet's greatest scenic antiquities could yet have been stayed, the man [Stewart Udall, then Secretary of the Interior] who theoretically had the power to save this place did not find a way to pick up a telephone and give the necessary order. I was within a few feet of his desk in Washington that day and witnessed how the forces long at work finally had their way. So a steel gate dropped, choking off the flow in the canyon's carotid artery, and from that moment the canyon's life force ebbed quickly. A huge reservoir, absolutely not needed in this century, almost certainly not needed in the next, and conceivably never to be needed at all, began to fill (1963: 7).

Brower's epitaph for Glen Canyon was countered by Floyd Dominy, Commissioner of the U.S. Bureau of Reclamation at the time Glen Canyon Dam was built:

To have a deep blue lake, Where no lake was before, Seems to bring man, A little closer to God. There is a natural order in our universe. God created both man and nature. And man serves God. But nature serves man. . . . [In Glen Canyon] man has flung down a giant barrier in the path of the turbulent Colorado . . . It has tamed the wild river— made it a servant to man's will. [It is now] a place where once remote wonders such as Rainbow Bridge are accessible . . . to everyone. . . . If I sound partisan toward Lake Powell, you are correct. I am proud of this aquatic wonder and want to share it with you (1964: 2).

While the great lake, with all its vast recreation potential, and the hydroelectric power produced by the dam's generators, are counted as gains, much was lost. The late Eliot Porter mourned the loss of the unique and unrivaled scenery in the place that had been Glen Canyon in his magnificent verbal and pictorial tribute, *The Place No One Knew: Glen Canyon on the Colorado*:

Remember these things lost. The native wildlife; the chance to float quietly down a calm river, to let the current carry you past a thousand years of history, through a living canyon of incredible, haunting beauty. Here the Colorado had created a display that rivaled any in the world. The side canyons simply had no rivals. We lost wholeness, integrity in a place, one that might always have let man experience a magnificent gesture of the natural world. No man, in all the generations to be born of man, will ever be free to discover for himself one of the greatest places of all. This we inherited, and have denied to all others—the place no one knew well enough (1963: 178).

Much else was lost, as well. Between 1957 and 1962, teams of researchers from the University of Utah and the Museum of Northern Arizona, at Flagstaff, labored in Glen Canyon trying to learn as much as was possible about its geology, ecology, archaeology, ethnohistory and history. They did not come to know it "well enough," but they came to know it as best they could. They were there under federal mandate, to "salvage" as much scholarly information as possible about Glen Canyon the place, and about those sojourners who were in and around the place over three millennia and more.

All the sojourners knew something about the place themselves, and lived and worked in it for various reasons. Groups of Indian people hunted, and later farmed, in and around the canyon over several millennia until about 1300. After about 1850, Navajo people herded livestock in the canyon. Beginning with Powell, in 1869, Whites explored it, went broke seeking gold in its sands and oil in its rocks, planned to build a railroad through it, ran its rapids and gazed in awe at its sublime grandeur, and tried futilely to describe that grandeur in mere words. The stories of all these sojourners were written by the teams of scholars who were in and around Glen Canyon in the 1950s and early 1960s, and other scholars who have been there since. (See Lindsay *et al.*, 1968, and Heib, 1996, on Glen Canyon archaeology.)

In the Fall of 1962, the late Professor Jesse D. Jennings began the first of what proved to be several attempts to summarize the discoveries made during the "salvage" research program. He finally got it right, according to his lights, on the fourth try. His *Glen Canyon: An Archaeological Summary*, now happily reprinted here, interprets and places into context information collected by the teams of archaeologists and ecologists who worked in Glen Canyon, its side-canyons, and the adjacent highlands. The pioneering historical studies of the canyon made by the late C. Gregory Crampton and others, as part of the larger salvage program, are summarized elsewhere (Crampton, 1965, 1988).

The research program was a function of the Upper Colorado River Basin Archaeological Salvage Program, of which the Glen Canyon Project, conducted by the University of Utah and the Museum of Northern Arizona, was the principal component. It is useful to place the Glen

Canyon Project in historical perspective, since it and similar projects were adjunct endeavors that generated those "forces long at work," which David Brower and other environmentalists regard as calumnious.

In some senses, John Wesley Powell might be held responsible for the dropping of the steel gate at the Glen Canyon damsite in 1963, thus closing the diversion tunnel through which the Colorado River waters were shunted while the dam was being constructed. When Powell came to the West after the Civil War, he saw that water was a scarce resource and that its control and allocation through irrigation was the key to the development of the land. Powell made all this clear in his famed *Arid Lands Report*, published in 1878 . In subsequent years, he labored mightily within the structure of the federal government to achieve the means for water control and land use, that is, a rational, federally-mandated reclamation policy for the American West. He was ridiculed and forced out of the Directorship of the U.S. Geological Survey for his attempts to curb, and give order and rationality to, the rampant exploitation of the West. Only in the last few months of his life did Powell see the beginnings of a federal reclamation policy with the creation of the Reclamation Service in 1902. But that policy, and actions flowing from that policy, went far beyond what Powell had envisioned, and in ways he probably would not have condoned.

Powell's focus was on intrariver-basin development and reclamation, similar to what the Mormons had achieved in nineteenth century Utah. He did not foresee large-scale generation of hydro-electric power nor the wholesale exportation of water from one river basin into another, both of which became major features of federal reclamation efforts. Nor, probably, did he foresee the enormous scale at which reclamation projects would be conceived and constructed in the twentieth century. By 1920, plans were well under way for massive dams to totally control all Western river basins, and ultimately all those rivers collectively draining the basin of the Mississippi River as well. Interestingly, the architect of the plan to control the Colorado River Basin was Arthur Powell Davis, Powell's nephew, whom he had hired in the 1880s as a topographical assistant in the U.S. Geological Survey. By the 1920s, Arthur Powell Davis was Commissioner of the Bureau of Reclamation and world renowned as a designer of high dams and massive reclamation projects in America, Europe, and Asia.

John Wesley Powell might also be held responsible for the "adjunct endeavors," as we have called them, which produced the scientific and historical data summarized herein by Professor Jennings. Powell managed to get the Bureau of Ethnology (after 1894 the Bureau of American Ethnology) established by the U.S. Congress in 1879 as an anthropological research arm of the Smithsonian Institution. He thus legitimized federal support for anthropological (including archaeological) studies throughout the United States. The federal Antiquities Act of 1906, designed to preserve, protect, and study archaeological sites and monuments on public lands, gave the Smithsonian Institution a key oversight role in those tasks.

In 1922, an extensive series of federally funded and designed water control projects were begun in the various river basins feeding into the Mississippi. These included a major dam at Muscle Shoals, Alabama. Officials at the Smithsonian and archaeologists at various universities argued that this project, and similar federal "actions," would result in the destruction of archaeological and historical sites by drowning them beneath the lakes behind the dams. Archaeological sites were and still are regarded as containers of scientific data; those data are revealed by proper scientific excavation and recording. If the sites were drowned before they were studied, the data they contained would be lost as well. Thus, the argument ran, it was incumbent upon the federal government to provide funds in support of archaeological "salvage" projects prior to the inundation of areas in which sites were found. While the site areas would be lost, the information they contained would be "salvaged" and ultimately made available to the general public through publications, museum displays, and the like. Thus, salvage archaeology became a matter of the public good and public interest. Congress and the construction agencies agreed, at first somewhat unwillingly, to this argument. Over time, as federal projects, especially large-scale dams, were approved and begun, a system of "salvage archaeology" was developed. Federal funds were made available through the construction agencies, and various museums and universities undertook the research on a contract basis. Many projects were carried out during the Depression years of the 1930s under the auspices of various agencies, such as the Works Progress Administration, especially in the Tennessee Valley, the Columbia River Basin, and in the building of Boulder (later Hoover) Dam on the Colorado River.

In 1935, Congress passed the Historic Sites Act, the legal cornerstone of all subsequent federal historic preservation (including archaeology) policy and legislation. The act gave the National Park Service "lead agency" status in preservation matters, including the administration of salvage archaeology projects. Henceforth, most federal funds to support such projects were channeled through the Park Service. During the 1930s Dr. Jennings was on the Park Service staff and was intimately familiar with the process as it evolved. After the Second World War, federal agencies dusted off a multitude of dam and reservoir, road, pipeline, highway, and other projects that so transformed the United States between the late 1940s and the early 1980s. Between 1960 and 1992, a plethora of federal legislative acts and presidential executive orders was put in place to structure and direct all federal preservation efforts, including archaeology. In the context of the new environmental awareness of the early 1970s, "salvage archaeology" gave way to "cultural resources management" as appropriate federal buzz-words, but the intent remained: to preserve and make available information about the past threatened by federal, or federally-funded, "undertakings" (Fowler, 1986).

The Glen Canyon Project was initiated under the Archaeological Salvage Program of the National Park Service as it had developed by the late 1950s. The procedure was simple and straightforward. Congress appropriated funds to the Bureau of Reclamation for the construction of the Glen Canyon Dam and ancillary facilities, including the bridge immediately downstream from the dam. The Bureau transferred a small percentage of those funds to the National Park Service for salvage archaeology and related studies. The Park Service in turn contracted, through annually-renewed Memoranda of Agreement, with the University of Utah (UU) and the Museum of Northern Arizona (MNA) to undertake the work. At the Museum of Northern Arizona in Flagstaff, William Y. Adams, Alexander Lindsay, Jr., and their associates developed a research and logistics plan for their portion of the project. At Utah, Professor Jennings developed a somewhat different plan, as he explains in the *Summary*. He primarily used graduate students as field crew-chiefs and undergraduates as assistants, hence the field season had to be tailored to the academic school year.

When the Glen Canyon Project began in 1957, there were a number of other fairly large-scale salvage archaeology projects under way in various parts of the United States, especially along the Missouri and Columbia rivers. They were all overseen by the Park Service and funded through it from Congress. The Glen Canyon Project, however, was different, principally because of the logistics required to get into, and live and work in, the main canyon, its tributaries, and the country they drained. Glen Canyon was "the place no one knew" for a reason—it was extremely difficult of access. In many places, to get from one canyon rim to the opposite rim directly across the river—a linear distance of a mile or less—required a vehicle trip of 400 to 500 miles or more, if there were any roads at all on the other side. Wooden boats and

World War II surplus rubber rafts provided transport on the river proper, but they could only be launched, or hauled out, at two points that were 160 river miles apart. Access to the upper reaches of the side canyons was primarily from the canyons' heads, via jeep, on horse- or mule-back, or on foot.

During the 1958 field season, the University of Utah river crew traveled twenty to fifty miles downstream by boat and one hundred miles by truck to the nearest supply point at Kanab, Utah—reversing the process to go back to work. Helicopters were available, but their operation and maintenance were prohibitively expensive and their use impractical in archaeology projects, except in dire emergencies. The MNA teams had similar logistics problems. Both teams used boats, jeeps, horses, mules and shoe-leather for travel.

Professor Jennings notes the logistics problems in his *Summary*. However, his detailed planning and the procedures he imposed on his crews are best seen in the discussion of the Glen Canyon Project in his autobiography, *Accidental Archaeologist*, published in 1994. Therein, he noted that the project "promised to be a tremendous research and student training opportunity that would come only once in a lifetime" (205). The opportunity was tempered by the complexities of working in the (then) very difficult country. His plans and procedures can be summarized in one quintessential Jennings maxim: "Only fools have adventures." That is, proper planning and proper implementation of those plans keep researchers healthy and able to produce and preserve sound scientific data. Put another way, the Glen Canyon Project was *not* a "wilderness adventure"—it was a carefully calculated and implemented scientific research project made more interesting by the logistical challenges involved. For those of us who were part of the project, Dr. Jennings's planning allowed us to meet the logistical challenges, get the research done on time and within budget, and remain healthy the while. Professionally and personally, the project was for each of us the opportunity of a lifetime as well.

Commenting on the project after three decades, Dr. Jennings confessed that he felt himself under great tension every field season when the crews were out and communication was minimal to non-existent. But his plans and procedures kept us from doing very much that was foolish. In retrospect, Dr. Jennings concluded that the project had been a success. "The Glen Canyon experience was all that I had expected and more. Scientifically it was a success in several ways" (1994: 215). A few random statistics provide a gauge of its success. The project lasted six years. It cost about one million dollars (later, and smaller, projects cost up to twenty times as much). At least 205 persons were on the payrolls of the two institutions for varying periods of time, including twenty-six members of the Navajo Nation. Between 1957 and 1966, 161 published monographs and technical papers put the project results on record. Of the more than 200 employees, most were students. At least thirty-six subsequently earned Ph.D.s, and another ten to twelve earned master's degrees; all those went on to anthropology careers in universities, museums, federal service or environmental consulting firms. Still others earned doctorates in history, biology, geology—and one in astrophysics.

Again in retrospect, Professor Jennings felt that the scientific contribution made by his *Summary*, together with the data from both institutions that back up his conclusions, increased understanding of prehistoric Anasazi lifeways. The several Anasazi subcultures, especially Kayenta, Mesa Verde, and Chaco, are the most studied archaeological cultures in the New World. Since the early 1960s, the amount of new research on the Anasazi and related cultures has resulted in an enormous explosion of data, hypotheses, and new insights, best summarized in Linda Cordell's magisterial *Archaeology of the Southwest* (1997). This explosion was just beginning in the early 1960s when Dr. Jennings wrote the *Summary*. The major idea he advanced in it has since permeated archaeological thinking about the Anasazi. As you read it, you will see the evidence being marshalled in support of the idea. Again from the perspective of three decades, Jennings wrote,

> . . . my argument [was] that the emphasis on the big late ruins and the accompanying elaborate crafts (pottery, textiles and lapidary work) [of the Anasazi subcultures] had tended to distort the true genius of the culture, which had been created and developed by many generations of small farmers who harvested many wild foods and skillfully exploited scant water resources near small areas of rich arable soil. They were essentially desert foragers who had learned to farm both wild and domesticated plants (1994: 216).

Rereading the summary in the light of present-day knowledge as presented by Dr. Cordell, this seemingly simple statement pithily epitomizes how most of the Anasazi and other puebloan folk lived in the Southwest for most of the period between about 1000 B.C.E. to 1300 C.E.

Finally, reading the summary also gives one some sense of Jennings the professor—a man with a no nonsense, straightforward, marshall-the-facts-and-state-a-conclusion approach to long-ago life and times in a place called Glen Canyon. Professor Jennings did work, and write, in that style. But Glen Canyon had its personal effect on him, as it did on all of us who worked there:

> On the personal side, learning the Glen and working in and near it for six or seven summers was a rich, emotionally charged period of my life. The vastness, the isolation, the stillness, the overwhelming beauty of the land, even (especially) the heat, the still starlit nights, the blue or brassy midday sky, all combined to make me constantly aware of my good fortune. To be sure, I never forgot that it was a dangerous land and that poor judgment or forgetting the water could bring disaster. However, if one accepted the conditions and respected them, it was a privilege as well as a challenge to have seen it and worked in it and returned with indelible, pleasant memories. In retrospect, to coin a phrase—tension or not—I fear I loved every minute of it (1994: 216-17).

Professor Jesse Jennings died in November, 1997, full of years and the awards brought by a brilliant six-decade career as teacher, administrator, researcher, and most importantly, "dirt archaeologist," the ultimate accolade within the profession. In my last conversation with him, shortly before his death, we spoke of Glen Canyon. He reiterated that planning and implementing the Glen Canyon Project was, in many ways, the high point of his career. We reminisced about the place both of us knew—but never knew well enough. What we—he and I and two hundred others—learned about the lives and times of some of the sojourners in Glen Canyon over about a 1300 year period, is summarized herein for all of us by Dr. Jennings and for a new generation who know only Lake Powell and wonder about what lies beneath it.

March 1, 1998.

Further Reading

Note: In addition to the publications cited in the foreward, some other useful sources are included in the following list. Collectively they convey the many different ways in which Glen Canyon itself, and those who sojourned there up through the construction of the dam, have been seen and interpreted since Powell's first explorations in 1869.

Abbey, Edward
    1968 *Desert Solitaire: A Season in the Wilderness.* Simon & Schuster, New York.
———.
    1971 *Slickrock: Endangered Canyons of the Southwest.* Sierra Club/Scribner's Sons, New York.
———.
    1975 *The Monkey Wrench Gang.* Lippincott, Philadelphia.
———.
    1982 *Down the River.* E. P. Dutton, New York.
Berger, Bruce
    1994 *There Was a River. Essays on the Southwest.* University of Arizona Press, Tucson.
Brower, David
    1963 Foreword. In *The Place No One Knew. Glen Canyon on the Colorado,* by Eliot Porter, pp. 7–10. Sierra Club, San Francisco.
Carrier, Jim, and Jim Richardson
    1992 *The Colorado. A River at Risk.* Westcliff Publications, Englewood, Colo.
Cordell, Linda
    1997 *Archaeology of the Southwest,* 2nd edition. Academic Press, New York.
Crampton, C. Gregory
    1965 *Standing Up Country. The Canyon Lands of Utah and Arizona.* Alfred L. Knopf, New York and University of Utah Press, Salt Lake City.
———.
    1988 *Ghosts of Glen Canyon. History Beneath Lake Powell.* Publishers Place, St. George, Utah.
Dominy, Floyd
    1964 *Lake Powell: Jewel of the Colorado.* U.S. Bureau of Reclamation, Washington, D.C.
Fowler, Don D. and Catherine S. Fowler (editors)
    1968 John Wesley Powell's Journal: Colorado River Exploration 1871–1872. *The Smithsonian Journal of History* 3(2): 1–44.
Geib, Phil R.
    1996 *Glen Canyon Revisited.* University of Utah Anthropological Papers 119. Salt Lake City.

Jennings, Jesse D.
   1994 *Accidental Archaeologist. Memoirs of Jesse D. Jennings.* University of
      Utah Press, Salt Lake City.
Lindsay, Alexander J., Jr., J. Richard Ambler, Muriel A. Stein and Philip M. Hobler
   1968 *Survey and Excavation North and East of Navajo Mountain, Utah,*
      1959–1962. Museum of Northern Arizona Bulletin no. 45, Flagstaff.
Martin, Russell
   1989 *A Story that Stands like a Dam. Glen Canyon and the Struggle for the*
      Soul of the West. Henry Holt & Co., New York.
McPhee, John
   1971 *Encounters with the Archdruid.* Farrer, Straus & Giroux, New York.
National Park Service
   1950 *A Survey of the Recreational Resources of the Colorado River Basin.*
      U.S. Dept. of the Interior, Washington, D.C.
Porter, Eliot
   1963 *The Place No One Knew. Glen Canyon on the Colorado.* Sierra Club,
      San Francisco.

   ————.

   1969 The Canyons of the Colorado—Past and Present 1969. In *Down the*
      Colorado. John Wesley Powell. Diary of the First Trip Through the
      Grand Canyon, pp. 149–63. E. P. Dutton, New York.
Powell, John Wesley
   1964 *Canyons of the Colorado.* Argosy-Antiquarian Ltd., New York. Origi-
      nally published in 1895.

   ————.

   1969 *Down the Colorado. John Wesley Powell. Diary of the First Trip*
      Through the Grand Canyon. Photographs and Epilogue by Eliot Porter,
      Foreword and Notes by Don D. Fowler. E. P. Dutton, New York.
      Reprinted 1988 by Arrowood Press, New York.
Stone, Julius F.
   1932 *Canyon Country. The Romance of Drop of Water and a Grain of Sand.*
      G. P. Putnam's Sons, New York.
Waters, Frank
   1946 *The Colorado.* Rinehart & Co., New York.
Webb, Roy
   1994 *Call of the Colorado.* University of Idaho Press, Moscow.

Preface

Jesse D. Jennings

The writing of this paper has been difficult. At yearly intervals since 1962 I have attempted it, and annually have discarded the abortive result. The problem was to find a meaningful approach. Merely to condense descriptive material would not only be redundant, but would depreciate the integrity and merit of the scores of monographs and papers already written about Glen Canyon findings. Or, one could produce a statement of the local region, generalizing on a descriptive level from the available reports, bolstering the whole with interminable trait lists and charts of occurrence. Such a paper would have been uninteresting either to write or to read. Finally, however, I hit upon the notion of commenting upon the value the program might have for other prehistorians, as well as the effect the data had upon my own views. Given this approach, whatever was said ought, I supposed, be kept brief. Should students of American prehistory require an assessment of the overall project, such a need could, one would hope, be satisfied with few words.

What follows is the fourth attempt. It is loosely structured and not highly particular, yet documented to permit further pursuit of the data by interested readers. (The bibliography contains all the publications resultant from the Upper Colorado River Basin studies known to me, whether cited in the text or not.)

The final form was much modified by others and it is a pleasure to acknowledge the value of advice, discussion and criticism I received specifically from Erik K. Reed, Charlie R. Steen, Albert H. Schroeder, Floyd W. Sharrock, C. Melvin Aikens, E. B. Danson, Alexander Lindsay, Kent Day and Kimball T. Harper, to say nothing of informal debate of minor and major points with Robert H. Lister, Warren d'Azevado, Robert C. Euler, and many students.

To the scores of participants in the Glen Canyon Archaeological Salvage Project, both with the University of Utah and the Museum of Northern Arizona, I can only proffer thanks for their loyalty and labor. The list follows.

Glen Canyon, University of Utah: P. O. Ackley and Associates, Herbert L. Alexander, Jr., Darrell Alvey, Edson Alvey, Forrest Alvey, Freeman Alvey, J. Richard Ambler, Ardelle Anderson, Kathryn Anderson, Keith Anderson, John F. Baldi, Tyler Bastian, Gail C. Bailey, Paul O. Benson, Joseph Bernolfo, Peter Bodenheimer, Tim Bradford, T. Jim Bradley, Tom Brockman, W. Donald Brumbaugh, Larry Bryant, Clifford G. Bryner, William Buckles, Audrey Buell, Bill Byers, Lynne Campbell, Robert Cheel, Susan Clark, Dan Coleman, Johnny Conway, Vard Coombs, Wayne Coon, R. Heward Courtney, Peter H. Cousins, Walter P. Cottam, C. Gregory Crampton, Leland H. Creer, Don D. Croft, Hugh Cutler, Edwin Dallin, M. E. Davis, Nolan Dean, John R. Dewey, David S. Dibble, Stephen Durrant, Frank Eddy, Margaret Eliason, Dick Ellis, Alice E. Aikens, Mabel Endo, Don Fowler, Vance J. Fowler, Seville Flowers, Ludell Fromme, Dorothy Frost, Everett Frost, Joyce Gardner, Loyd Gates, Mike Gibbons, J. R. Gipson, John Glaser, Richard Gould, Richard K. Graham, Bob Grant, Cicil Griffin, Lamon Griffin, Gordon L. Grosscup, Ray Groussman, James H. Gunnerson, Vasyl M. Gvosdetsky, Ethel C. Hale, Kathleen Halverson, Gale Hammond, Lyndon L. Hargrave, James Haug, Charles F. Hayes III, Elaine Hendricks, Nancy Hewitt, Harry P. Hewitt, Matt Hill, Keith Hottinger, Allen Howard, Jeff B. Hulen, Wilfred Husted, Robert Jager, J. David Jennings, Jr., Herbert Jennings, Russell C. Jensen, George Jones, Joseph Jorgensen, Lawrence Kaplan, Edward G. Keane, Kate P. Kent, George King, A. D. Koloseike, Carl Kuehne, John Kuzara, Chester Lay, M. Raymond Lee, June F. Lipe, William D. Lipe, Florence Lister, F. J. Lombard, Mark Lyman, Thomas Lynch, John F. Lance, Alan Matheson, Thomas W. Mathews, Donald R. Mathis, Mildred Mathias, John Merkeley, Ruth Meserve, Norma Mikkelsen, Marilyn Moore, Doyle Moosman, Kent B. Morgan, Jon Morris, Mary Mulroy, Jean S. Musser, J. L. Nelson, James L. Nichols, Robert F. Nichols, James Nielson, Rose Odette, Janet Owens, Bill Palmer, Lyle Palmer, Edna Pass, Leslie Pennington, Cal Porter, Weldon Porter, Caralee Price, John Price, Nancy A. Price, William Purdy, Lyle E. Pyeatt, Barry Quin, Dirk Raat, Downey Raibourn, David Read, Jay Redd, Clarence A. Reeder, Jr., Norman L. Ritchie, Lynn Arnold Robbins, Sterling Robbins, Sarah A. Robertson, Keith Rogers, Jerry Roundy, Richard Ross, T. Melvin Ross, Ernst Schurer, David Schwarts, J. Dan Scurlock, Alexander Sharp, Anna O. Shepard, Barbara Sibley, Charline G. Smith, Ted C. Smith, Ellen Sparry, Brigham Stevens, Peter Stiefel, Joseph Stocks, Carol J. Stout, M. Kent Stout, Dee Ann Suhm, Catherine L. Sweeney, Elsa Torres, Melanie Treacy, Mildred Treacy, Christy G. Turner II, Jane Turner, Oliver

Thomas, Mike Useem, Mike Valent, Dirk H. Vander Elst, Robert Walsh, Frank Weir, Ted Weller, Spencer Whitney, Norman C. Williams, Sylvia W. Willie, Lindsey Wilson, Wilford K. Wiseman, Robert Wissmar, Carl Woolsey, Warren Woolsey, Frank Wright, Angus Woodbury, W. C. Wright, Midori Yamaguchi, F. J. Zarecor.

Glen Canyon, Museum of Northern Arizona: Nettie K. Adams, William Y. Adams, J. Richard Ambler, Thomas G. Bowen, J. W. Bower, Bryant Bannister, John S. Belmont, Kenneth A. Bennett, Katharine Bartlett, Stanley Beus, David A. Bonderman, William J. Breed, David A. Breternitz, W. H. Carrington, Harold S. Colton, Maurice E. Cooley, C. Gregory Crampton, Hugh Cutler, Calvin R. Cummings, Jeffrey S. Dean, Dorothy M. Diehl, Nancy D. Epler, Robert C. Euler, Gene Foster, Marc Gaede, Xerpha Gaines, Elizabeth A. Galligan, Philip M. Hobler, May Fleming, Lyndon A. Hargrave, Inez M. Haring, Thomas P. Harlan, Horace S. Haskell, Loren R. Haury, Stephen D. Hayden, Ada T. Hatch, C. Nicolas Hawkes, Angelita Hernandez, Charles Kearns, Kate Peck Kent, Roger E. Kelly, Jr., Joseph Kirby, Jane L. King, Jarvis R. Klem, Caesar T. Lee, Alexander J. Lindsay, Jr., Faye Long, Paul V. Long, Jr., Walter B. McDougall, Robert L. McGregor, Otis Marston, Frank E. Masland, Jr., Jane Metzger, William C. Miller, Michael E. Moseley, Carol Murphy, Alan P. Olson, Edward E. B. Perin, Roxine M. Phillippi, William J. Robinson, John P. Schreiber, Robert Sears, David Smith, Lydia Solberg, Mary Anne Stein, Jarvis D. Swannack, Jr., Dennis E. Tedlock, Christy G. Turner II, Milton A. Wetherill, Barton A. Wright, J. Frank Wright, Lyn Wright.

Navajo Indians: Kid C. Atene, Harry Bitsinne, John Bryant, Etta Chief, Ferl Chief, Kee Yazzi Clitso, Ephraim Crank, Tom Dougi, Eugene Holgate, Kee Bahe Holiday, Bahe Ketchum, Dana King, Fannie King, Ned King, Willie King, Floyd Laughter, Clyde Little, Buck Navajo, Tom Navajo, Dan Lehi, Ivan Nelson, Jimmie Nelson, Jack Owl, Toby Owl, Delbert Smallcanyon, Buck Whitehat.

It will be noted that there is some overlap of personnel between the two institutions. The Navajo tribesmen are cited separately in order to highlight their effective participation in the activity.

All illustrations, unless otherwise credited come from University of Utah Glen Canyon files or were specially drafted for this report.

Although I have elsewhere mentioned this, I wish again to mention the pleasure I've experienced during the years of Glen Canyon project operation with the National Park Service. Especially I mention Herbert E. Kahler, John M. Corbett, Charlie R. Steen and Erik K. Reed whose tolerance, understanding and awareness have been able to absorb the

xxiv

human frailties and consequent delays and disappointments which developed during the prosecution of the program.

With great appreciation I mention the patience and skill of Jane C. Jennings and Norma Mikkelsen in checking bibliography, grammar and form.

Finally, I am well aware that *Glen Canyon: A Summary* could have taken a hundred forms. This is the one which seemed to me appropriate (and comfortable) and it will, I hope, be helpful to others.

1966

Glen Canyon Archaeology: A Summary

Introduction

For eight seasons—from 1956 through 1963—research in several fields of science was carried on under emergency conditions in the Glen Canyon area, largely in Utah, of the Colorado River in response to the threat of losses posed by the construction of Glen Canyon Dam in northern Arizona. This area lies within the region known as the Canyon Lands Section of the Colorado Plateau. Here study was concentrated on archaeology, ethnohistory, geology, history, paleontology, and various aspects of biology. Ancillary to the broader studies, there were limited exercises in palynology, sedimentation, ethnobotany, dendrochronology and human ecology. Until this time, no previous emergency project had encompassed a spectrum of science so broad nor enlisted the aid of a corps of specialists so diversified. By 1965, however, the approach used in the Glen Canyon has verged upon the commonplace (e.g., MacNeish, 1964; Osborne, et al., 1965).

The ideal summary of the work of this host of specialists, all obliquely concerned with human history, would be a grand synthesis wherein all findings were integrated into what might be called "The Natural History of the Glen Canyon Area." In some ways this account *is* natural history because human behavior is not only tied to the resources—physiographic, biotic and climatic—of a land, but all these are in some degree modified (or modifiable) by human behavior, and man is a vital force in nature. Thus, this report will verge upon what might be called human paleoecology, long a concern of prehistorians.

A summary should also recapitulate achievements and set forth the net effect of the finds as they either change, modify or confirm previous conclusions and interpretations. Particular attention should be devoted to fitting the research into the larger scientific frameworks where the major contributions fall, or as these have significance on somewhat

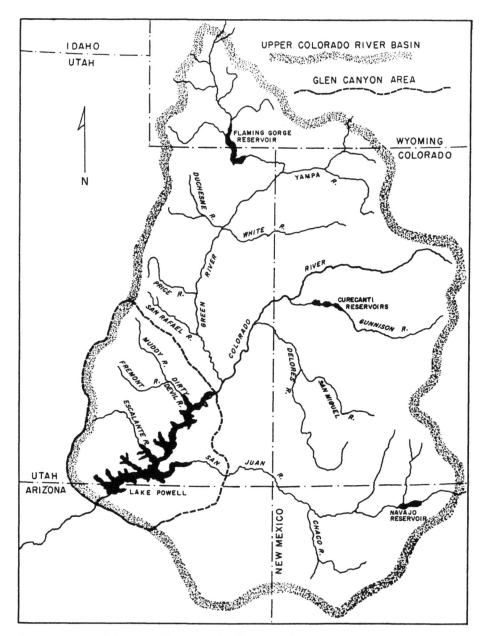

Fig 1. System of dams and lakes in the Upper Colorado River Basin. (Derived from A. Woodbury, *et al.*, 1959a; Jennings, 1961.)

higher levels than as mere accretions to a corpus of data. And above all a summary should summarize, not repeat. Fortunately most of the raw data are already available in published form, so relatively little new material need be introduced here.

History

This project, like all other human affairs, has a unique story of its own and this background should be reviewed in order that the circumstances surrounding the study can be understood. The Glen Canyon studies are tied to a larger program that was developed to prevent scientific losses caused by the construction of several dams and the lakes these dams created in the Upper Colorado River Basin (Fig. 1). Since Powell's pioneering trip of 1869, the Colorado River has symbolized the ultimate in romance, danger and adventure as its famous canyons—especially the Grand—became household words. But the river's challenge was felt by engineers and farmers and politicians as well as by white-water men and river runners, and the lower river was long ago tamed by Hoover, Parker and Davis dams. At these locations electricity is generated as the stored waters are released and diverted to irrigate huge tracts of land and to provide life for thirsty west coast cities. Harnessing the upper part of the Colorado River system—that part upstream from Lees Ferry—was not undertaken until 1956, when the construction of four dams was authorized. These four dams, key structures in a complex master scheme, were Flaming Gorge in northeastern Utah, Curecanti in western Colorado, Navajo in northwest New Mexico, and Glen Canyon in Arizona. Scientific study was carried out in each reservoir area through the Upper Colorado River Basin Archeological Salvage Project, an activity sponsored and supervised by the National Park Service of the Department of the Interior. Research was conducted, however, by four contracting agencies: The University of Colorado, the University of Utah, the Museum of Northern Arizona and the Museum of New Mexico.

No basinwide coordination of research strategy was attempted. For each of three reservoir areas there was one major contractor who designed the research and operated the undertaking as local circumstances, problems and conditions warranted. For the Glen Canyon project, fourth and largest of all, two contractors were involved: the University of Utah and the Museum of Northern Arizona. (The University of Utah also undertook study of the Flaming Gorge and Fontenelle reservoir areas.) Assigned different areas (Fig. 2) and guided by differ-

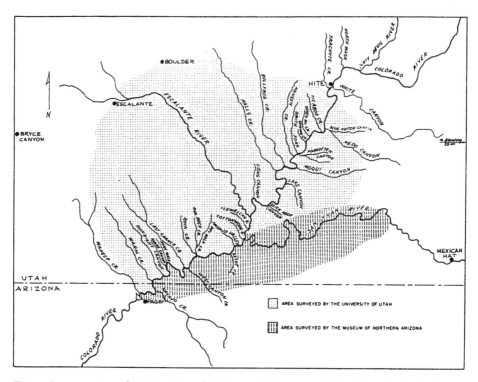

Fig 2. Areas assigned University of Utah and Museum of Northern Arizona for Glen Canyon Project. (Derived from Lister, 1959a; Lipe, 1958.)

ent research designs, the institutions entered into no formal coordination of field work or other phases of study, but continuous informal exchange of data and information at all levels provided an effective, if unstructured, coordination of the research. There was casual contact between the two Glen Canyon contractors and the other two institutions—Museum of New Mexico at the Navajo Reservation and University of Colorado at Curecanti—during the occasional conferences called by the responsible National Park Service officials. These latter conferences, primarily concerned with exchange of data, findings and preliminary interpretations were exceedingly helpful to all contractors. Although this report is concerned only with Glen Canyon, with no further reference to the larger Upper Colorado River Basin program, except as findings there are relevant in later interpretive statements, the Glen Canyon work must still be understood as only part of the larger Upper Colorado River Basin enterprise.

Initiation of the emergency program followed the passage of the basic legislation (Federal Public Law 485) by the second session of the 85th Congress. Long before passage of the bill (approved April 11, 1956) the National Park Service was alert to the problem, long since become routine, of the need to salvage the scientific values placed in jeopardy by the proposed construction. The Park Service's action in the matter is authorized by the Historic Sites Act of 1935 which charges the Secretary of the Interior, through the National Park Service, among other things with the responsibility for preservation of antiquities. With Glen Canyon Dam scheduled for immediate construction, the National Park Service began negotiation of contracts for emergency research by July of 1956. By January of 1957 a contract had been awarded to the Museum of Northern Arizona for the archaeology of the main stem of the Colorado, below the San Juan River and the left bank tributaries of the same stretch. The left bank of the San Juan and its tributaries were also included. Later, by informal agreement with the University of Utah, the entire San Juan system was handled by the Museum of Northern Arizona. The Museum of Northern Arizona was also assigned the detailed geological study aimed at rounding out the general geological data already available.

In June of 1957, the University of Utah assumed responsibility for the archaeology of the rest of the area as well as for historical and ecological research over the entire area. After these initial contracts—actually the contract was called a Memorandum of Agreement—funds were annually available (appropriated by the Congress in the national budget) through renewed Memoranda of Agreement. As time went on, University of Utah agreements came to include a survey of the Kaiparowits Plateau, a study of Southern Paiute ethnohistory, and numerous ancillary studies, while the Museum of Northern Arizona territory was extended to the highlands south of the river—Paiute and Cummings mesas and Rainbow Plateau.

Although the results of all the above extensions enter importantly into later substantive sections of this report, even more important was their stimulus on University of Utah research in other portions of the Southwest where comparative material, necessary to interpret Glen Canyon findings, was known or thought to occur. In this latter category of stimulated additional studies are the researches at the Coombs site near Boulder, Utah (Lister, et al., 1959–1961); excavations on the Kaiparowits Plateau (Fowler and Aikens, 1963); those near Kanab, Utah and in the vicinity of St. George, Utah (Aikens, 1965b); the latter location is over 100 airline miles westward from Glen Canyon Dam. These latter studies were made possible by grants in aid of research from the Wenner-Gren Foundation for Archeological Research, the University of Utah Research Fund and the National Science Foundation. Mention must also be made of volunteer labor from the University of Colorado summer students and St. Marks School for Boys in Salt Lake City. Also, through Bureau of Reclamation contracts, the ecological studies were much augmented during an evapotranspiration analysis of Glen Canyon vegetation. Out of all the contracts and the related research came the awareness that more information about the Fremont and Sevier Fremont of northern Utah was necessary; this study, recently initiated and still current, has National Science Foundation support. The last University of Utah Memorandum of Agreement bears the date of 15 July 1964, having been issued to cover the completing and publishing of a series of reports. (More historical detail can be found in Jennings, 1959b, 1961; Jennings and Sharrock, 1965; Adams and Adams, 1959; Adams, 1960).

The two contracting institutions, the University of Utah and the Museum of Northern Arizona, designed different research programs. The Museum of Northern Arizona, geared for decades to support of the traditional problem-oriented scholar, drew up a long range research program, allocated special space for project personnel and recruited graduate students for the professional staff. Research assistants were recruited from high school, undergraduate and graduate students as well as from the Navajo tribe.

At the University of Utah, where teaching must come first, no previous pattern fit the new conditions. Earlier research in prehistory had been a byproduct of teaching—archaeological summer field schools were conducted from 1949 through 1956—with the analysis of the data being done by students or staff members as individual research projects. Additionally, a continuing statewide survey was a function of the Department of Anthropology at the University of Utah. But it was apparent that the contract called for more than the standard and leisurely pattern. Consequently it was decided to create a research organization as a separate activity, subordinate to the statewide survey which in turn was a function of the departmental concern with archaeological research. The design envisioned a separate full time research staff freed from teaching and administrative duties, occupying separate and fully equipped quarters with part-time research assistants available for laboratory and technical tasks (e.g., a photographer, draftsman, records clerk). Published reports were to be predominantly descriptive, and were to be kept current with field work, intended to appear within 12 months after each field season ended.

In partial implementation of these aims, a central processing laboratory was established to operate separately in support of field research. The supervising field archaeologists were recognized as controlling the quality of the research. A manual of standard laboratory and field procedures was drawn up and comprised a uniform system of recording of all classes of data. At all times, graduate and undergraduate students were to receive preference in all employment; this provision recognized the teaching/apprenticeship value of the entire operation which, along with student financial aid, alone justified its location on a campus as an integral part of an academic department. The details of the project design, the special limitations of emergency contact work and the several advantages of contract research are to be found in Jennings (1959b, 1963a) as well as in Wasley (1961) and Wendorf (1962). The design briefly outlined above left the establishment of year by year schedules, and the annual identification of pressing scientific problems (in fact, all planning) very flexible.

Conclusions

With the closing of the gates of Glen Canyon Dam in 1963, the field aspects of the emergency ended. At this writing (May, 1966) Lake Powell is one-third filled and has become a recreational resource for the nation, entirely obscuring the canyons where researchers worked in heat, dust and hardship. During 1965 Powell attracted boaters, fishermen, campers, water-skiers, and photographers to a total exceeding 250,000 persons.

An overwhelming aspect of the recreational success of Lake Powell is the stunning grandeur of its red-rock setting. Nowhere in the Americas do comparable features occur. Lake Powell (itself 183 miles long with 1800 miles of shoreline) lies slender and imprisoned between sheer cliffs and towering buttes. The vastness, desolation and beauty of the Glen, the main artery of the Canyon Lands Province, is only slowly grasped. The romantic appeal of the Canyon Lands derives from about equal parts of beauty, isolation, ruggedness and difficulty, and the lure of the dangerous unknown.

The Glen Canyon work reminds one that the randomness or arbitrariness of emergency archaeological assignments has great advantages. The emergency programs of the past two decades have advanced scholarship beyond anything "problem research" would perhaps ever have done. Of first importance in this development is the obligation that the salvage operations must sample *all* the cultures thrust into jeopardy within a specified area. This responsibility is buttressed by the equally important enforcement of careful work and reporting from large geographic areas where "problems" have never led, areas where the archaeological remains were of "no value" to the investigator who pursued some other "problem."

Because, among other things, salvage assignments do not develop as "problems," all emergency work for a time has suffered from a well defined and explicitly phrased onus. It was regarded as unclean because in a vague sense it was "applied" science, whereas problems were "pure." And, another point, touched perceptively but incompletely by Wasley (1961), should be a little further discussed. This is in the matter of new techniques which have reputedly arisen as a result of the pressures of emergency work.

Now as to the first point, one can easily assess the amount of new archaeological data since intensive salvage began in 1945. In Brew (1961) there is a reference to the major list, as of 1959, of publications of the salvage operations. The list totals about 300 entries. Jennings (1955) earlier lists a bibliography of 150 titles for the Plains alone. A glance at the literature for Oklahoma reveals that without WPA digs in the 1930's and recent emergency jobs, the prehistory of the state would still be unknown. In Missouri in the case of the Pomme de Terre Reservoir, the author, W. Raymond Wood (1961) is able to say:

> . . . In a sense, it was fortunate that this reservoir was constructed, since western Missouri had acquired a reputation as a lacklustre area which would discourage investigation. . . . Therefore there were two important objectives of the work in the reservoir. The first was to describe the cultural complexes . . . to adjoining areas.

Thus, through a sampling of representative sites selected from the 400 found during survey work, the salvage program in Pomme de Terre allowed the establishment of a regional sequence with well delineated connections outside the region; this from an area which would perhaps never have received systematic study because it was drab. A lengthy series of occupancies from Nebo Hill times up to historic Osage was found; new trait attributes for Nebo Hill, among others, were discovered.

As a further example of advances wholly resultant from salvage, I cite the work of Lehmer (1954a, b) in the Oahe Reservoir wherein he established new foci, outlined a discrete new archaeological area and ended by proffering not only an explanation of Plains prehistory, but an explanation which clarified the last 1000 years of Plains prehistory more economically and convincingly than had anything up to that time. Or again in Kansas, the mere survey of Tuttle Creek Reservoir established a sequence of 8–10,000 years where no such thing had been suspected. This is in addition to material of the Archaic stage and two sites yielding projectile points usually ascribed to an even earlier stage. That no follow-up work has been undertaken in the Kansas area does not discount the importance of the original discovery, a discovery which resulted from reservoir salvage survey.

Turning to the northwest, almost the entire body of prehistoric data results from salvage operations. Reference here of course to Cressman's (1960) work in the Dalles, and that of Shiner (1961) and Osborne, *et al.* (1961) in the Columbia Plateau. Among other things Cressman shows the probable existence of an early chopper-scraper horizon entirely unexpected in the region. And again Butler's (1965) outlining of an hypothetical Old Cordilleran is, whether finally sustained by the evidence or not, a function of salvage work and opens anew the question of the pre-projectile point stages which one must posit, on logical grounds, for the western world.

In the Plains, the most dramatic gains in knowledge are exemplified by Wedel's (1961) recent synthesis of Plains prehistory. This could not have been written any earlier; the data did not exist until the reservoir sampling salvage work began.

Perhaps the most dramatic documentation of my thesis that "problem" search can often, and repeatedly, get nowhere is seen in Adams's 1960) account of 90 years of research in Glen Canyon. Here, in a restrained way, he chronicles the history of over 30 major explorations of the Glen Canyon by problem oriented or pothunting men whose work resulted in no adequate scientific account. Indeed, so little was known of this sparsely settled region, but rumors were so rife, that the salvage operation here reviewed was necessary before the vast region could be certified as being understood well enough that inundation posed no threat of significant loss to science.

Turning to the other matter, emergency programs have been equally valuable in the freeing of technique from rote or ritual procedures and devices which have often actually hampered archaeological field work. One shibboleth is the injunction on young men that the "aim of the record is that one be able, if it is desired, to restore the site exactly as it was." This commandment has led to incredible feats of spurious accuracy. An east coast example is the plotting by transit bearing and depth below an arbitrary datumplane of every sherd, on every level, from a prolific site. Or, in other cases the slow brushing away of a site with trowels and the plotting of each scrap in a refuse midden or dump heap is comparably pointless. Or the 10,000 cramped hours which men have spent in alternate checkerboarded 5 foot squares slowly wearing away sterile fill with whisk brooms. Other examples of blind ritualistic excavation techniques, wasteful of time and funds, techniques without relevance in the specific context where used, will occur to readers. It is possible now to say that, under the pressure of emergency work, intelligent appraisal of the kinds and relevance or redundancy of the data to be recovered has often led to a selection of the appropriate techniques. Thus, the ritual technician has been often (not always)pushed aside to make room for one who achieves an intelligent marriage of tools to tasks. Wendorf (1962) makes an excellent statement about field techniques. Wasley (1961), although he is aware that "it would not be fair to claim that salvage archaeology has been responsible for the addition of many, if indeed any, specific tools to this (basic) inventory (of techniques)," does explicitly see "major contributions (that) lie in selecting and developing combinations of tools and techniques which increased the efficiency of field work." He also emphasizes the problem of time limit. However, one can say here that time and costs have always been a consideration in archaeological work. The problem is not new; it has merely been ignored or deemed beneath the notice of the true scholar.

Of course, I would argue that no, or very few, techniques were actually "pioneered" or developed in the face of emergency situations, but highly intelligent adaptation and flexible applications have been made, while a few refinements may have been added. The chief new ingredient in technique is intellectual, being seen in the excavator's willingness to use varied tools. In my attempts to teach field procedures I constantly enjoin students to always "use the coarsest tool which will do the work—i.e., recover the data." A shovel can be as useful as a trowel, a road patrol or scraper as useful as a shovel, or a dragline as useful as a pick, in the hands of an excavator who is free of ritual compulsiveness.

In view of the mountains of useful data recovered by emergency operations, of the inescapably superior quality of most of the extant reports and of the strides in scientific understanding achieved over vast areas of the land, it seems to me that "pure" scientists have been proved thoroughly wrong. In fact good archaeology can be, and has been, done in a variety of unfavorable situations. Archaeology is a complex of attitudes supported by a few simple field techniques and is always done in the face of some set of limiting factors—time, money, equipment, labor competence—to name a few. The use of practical intelligence in applying techniques usually results in good archaeology. Techniques alone, applied in sequence and by rote, frequently yield garbled culture history.

As a summary, I suggest that in virtually any detail, and certainly in overall results, emergency salvage archaeology is superior to most other work done in America except possibly that of Gila Pueblo where, in southern Arizona, total coverage resulted in the recognition of a deep sequence of occupation. The pendulum has swung to realistic adjustment of tools to the task, and the rejection of rote procedures. The volume of data recovered insures the consequent likelihood of fullest recovery of the range of physical specimens, and the possibility of discovery of nuances of relationship in the recovery of ancillary data (palynology, etc.) is greatly enhanced as well. Utilization of all these data in interpretation, bringing vast knowledge out of "unimportant" areas, is the accomplishment of many emergency programs. In some degree the same achievements can be claimed for the Glen Canyon researchers of the University of Utah, the Museum of Northern Arizona and the Museum of New Mexico.

The Setting

Geology

The Glen Canyon terrain results from about 300 million years of geologic process, extending deep into Paleozoic times. Taking the Colorado Plateau as a physiographic unit with several subdivisions, Hunt (1956) gives a concise synthesis of the complex history of the Plateau (Fig. 3) period by period. The Glen Canyon and the Upper Colorado Basin drainage system was born late in this story. Growth of the system from youth to maturity through two cycles can be read from the evidence summarized in graphic style in Fig. 3, h, i, j, taken from Hunt. What these maps tell is a story of the uplift and deformation of Paleozoic and Cenozoic sediments—mostly sandstone—deposited both by wind and water over western Colorado, most of Utah and much of Arizona and western New Mexico from the Carboniferous Period onward.

The present form of the Colorado River, and Glen Canyon results from two recent periods of down cutting. The drainage system developed and the streams matured during early Miocene times, over a period of 4 million years or more. Then in Middle Miocene times the Plateau was elevated so that drainage ceased and many areas ponded, but by late Pliocene times—no more than 5 million years ago—the streams were again occupied and their channels cut much more deeply into the older sediment. The typical cross-section of the stream channels of the Canyon Lands section, a section best seen in Glen, is shown in Fig. 4.

Topography

By virtue of these two cycles of down cutting, the Colorado River created a continuous cross-section of sediments up to 300 million years old; this same cross-section also reveals the warping, tilting and faulting of past epochs summarized in Figs. 5, 6, and 7.

Fig. 5 presents a simple diagram of the formations which formed the bed of Glen Canyon and those which comprise the walls of the channel.

Note the slight and even gradient of the river bed, and that the sediments exposed in the walls upstream are older than those in the downstream stretch. Fig. 6 shows the lithology and topographic expressions of the full sequence of sediments in the Glen Canyon area. The nature of the Canyon Lands section is inherent in the geology. It is a rugged tract of naked rock and sandy soils with miles of active dunes, sandstones much dissected by deeply incised tributary canyons flowing into the deep and sinuous Colorado, a young stream following an old stream bed (Fig. 7). In much of the Glen Canyon the cliffs of the river and the exposed bare rock above are of the Glen Canyon Group—Navajo, Kayenta and Wingate sandstones. All are richly colorful—Navajo being red, Kayenta, purple red, and Wingate, the oldest, an orange red. All erode easily, and Navajo and Wingate leave spectacular vertical cliffs, columns and buttes as well as large stripped bare rock areas. The stripped Navajo surfaces, particularly, are studded with domed remnants. Interesting attributes of the massive sandstones are 1) their vast cavate shell-like alcoves or caves which form in cliffs during downward erosion, and 2) their water collecting and storing properties. Beneath the Glen Canyon group, the Chinle is often exposed. This member is in part clayey and unstable, eroding easily from beneath the harder Wingate so that Chinle talus slopes are usually littered with huge spalls broken from the columnar and cliffy sandstone above (Figs. 8 and 9).

Climate

The climate of this broken country is characterized by extreme heat and aridity. It boasts no permanent settlements except where mining or other extractive enterprises require personnel. There are also some cattle ranging the area, tended on periodic visits by cowhands who reside in one or another of the nearby towns (Fig. 2).

In contrast to the uplands where living water is lacking (Ambler, *et al.*, 1964; Fowler and Aikens, 1963), several of the tributary canyons carry perennial streams fed by springs issuing from seams and faults in the Navajo member. These quiet side streams support a lush vegetation on or at the base of the rich sediments derived from the parent rocks. The cool, sweet water flows past stands of cottonwood and willow, under shaded fern-mantled cliffs. The canyons, cool and filled with bird and animal life, are in great contrast to the sere red wastes of the slick rock.

All the canyons have often been even more productive than now. As

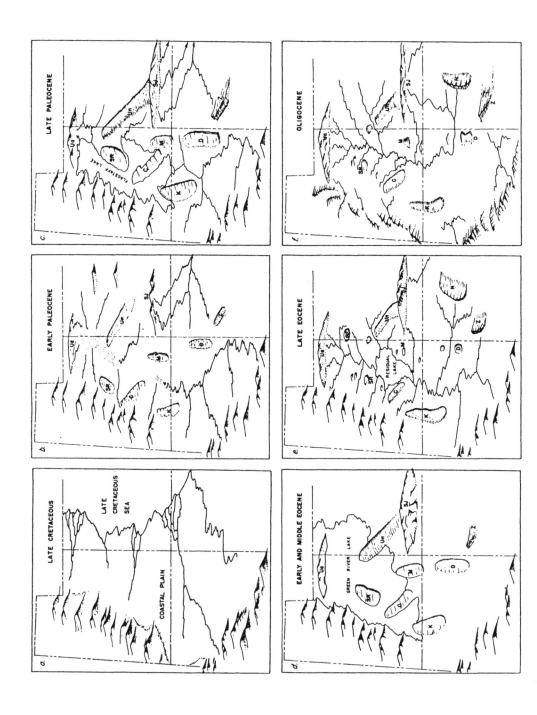

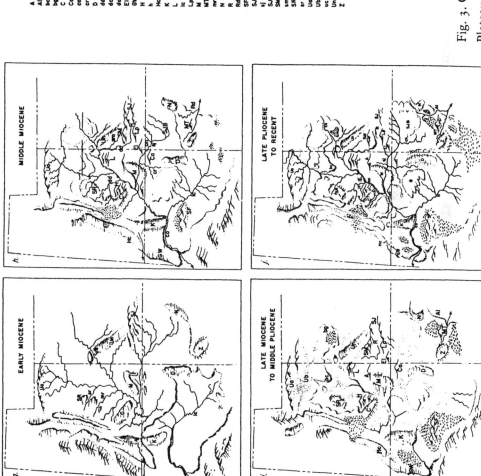

EXPLANATION

A   ABAJO MOUNTAINS
Al   ALAMOSA FAULT
bc   BOOK CLIFFS
bg   BATTLEMENT & GRAND MESAS
C   CIRCLE CLIFFS UPWARP
Ca   CARRIZO MOUNTAINS
co   COLORADO RIVER
cr   CHINLE CREEK
D   DEFIANCE UPWARP
dd   DIRTY DEVIL RIVER
dc   DOUGLAS CREEK ANTICLINE
do   DELORES RIVER
El   EL LATE MOUNTAIN
GW   GRAND WASH
H   HENRY MOUNTAINS
h   HALLS CREEK
Hc   HURRICANE CLIFFS
K   KAIBAB UPWARP
L   LA SAL MOUNTAINS
lc   LITTLE COLORADO RIVER
Lp   LA PLATA MOUNTAINS
M   MONUMENT UPWARP
MT   MOUNT TAYLOR
mr   MUDDY RIVER
N   NACIMIENTO MOUNTAINS
R   RICO DOME
Rd   RIO GRANDE DEPRESSION
SF   SAN FRANCISCO MOUNTAIN
SJ   SAN JUAN MOUNTAINS
sj   SAN JUAN RIVER
SJB SAN JUAN BASIN
SM   SAN MIGUEL MOUNTAINS
sm   SAN MIGUEL RIVER
SR   SAN RAFAEL SWELL
sr   SAN RAFAEL RIVER
Ua   UINTA MOUNTAINS
Ub   UINTA BASIN
uc   UNAWEEP CANYON
Un   UNCOMPAHGRE UPWARP
Z   ZUNI UPWARP

Fig. 3. Geological history of the Colorado Plateau. (Modified from Hunt, 1956).

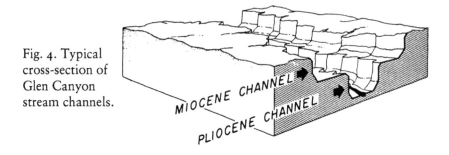

Fig. 4. Typical cross-section of Glen Canyon stream channels.

MIOCENE CHANNEL

PLIOCENE CHANNEL

recently as A.D. 1915 in some cases (Sharrock, *et al.*, 1961b) these deep narrow canyons contained rich sediments as deep as 90 feet, across which the clear streams meandered. With the high water table and the broad floor plain extending from cliff to cliff, each canyon supported the same varied fauna and flora but in larger quantity than now occurs. While today's streams all flow on bedrock between sheer rock walls, in every canyon the remnants of the earlier valley fill form crumbling earthen cliffs beside the stream. Some of the narrower channels have been flushed out entirely by local floods and the stains alone attest the earlier deep sediment. Aboriginally, then, the canyon floors were fertile soil, contrasting greatly with the present scene.

Ecology

The topography, climate and the qualities of the bedrock formations together exert powerful, if not complete, control over the biota of the Glen and its tributaries. Biota, for present purposes, must include man and whatever effect his exploitive measures may have had on the entire ecosystem. It is this latter point this chapter is addressed.

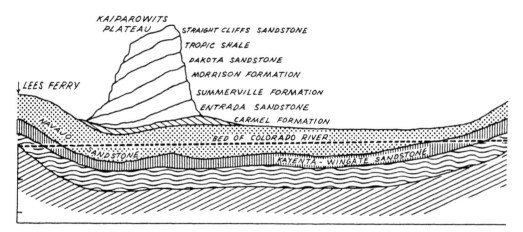

KAIPAROWITS PLATEAU
STRAIGHT CLIFFS SANDSTONE
TROPIC SHALE
DAKOTA SANDSTONE
MORRISON FORMATION
LEES FERRY
SUMMERVILLE FORMATION
ENTRADA SANDSTONE
CARMEL FORMATION
BED OF COLORADO RIVER
NAVAJO SANDSTONE
KAYENTA WINGATE SANDSTONE

Fig. 5. Cross-section of Glen Canyon formations from Lees Ferry to Hite. (Modified

17

As A. Woodbury and his associates (various) summarize the data, sharp zones of floral difference can be reduced to Fig. 10. The faunal boundaries cannot be quite so sharply drawn, but do show preference for or restriction to specific floral zones. Fig. 10 represents the channels below the slick rock rim of the old channel. Above the rim, depending on local conditions, there is no life on the slick rock, but where the sands and stabilized dunes have accumulated there are the same rain-dependent desert plants as found on the banks and slopes above the capillary and ground water zones of the canyons. The upland mesas have another distinctive plant assemblage, involving more precipitation and greater elevation.

In all the Glen Canyon area the annual precipitation nowhere exceeds 10 inches, except in mountains (e.g., Henry Mountains) or in the higher, distant plateaus (e.g., Kaiparowits). Most Plateau stations report less than 10 inches. This aridity is intensified by annual heat averages of 59.7° F. at Hite to 61.0° F. at Lees Ferry, with daytime summer heats routinely above 100° F. The canyon beds lie below 3500 feet elevation, with the plateaus ranging from 4500 to 7000 feet above sea level. As a result of these differences in elevation and the basic land forms, there exist 3 major environments and several variations on them; one is the arid *slick rock and dunes,* supporting little life. Second is the streamside-canyon environment dependent upon available soils, and water other than rainfall. Both of these two, moreover, comprise what are called desert condition. These lands, essentially those below 4500 feet elevation, are combined by Lindsay (writing in Ambler, *et al.,* 1964) and called the *lowlands, canyon lands* or *river environment.* The third environment is the higher wooded plateaus, where pinon, juniper and sage attest heavier rainfall. These, above 4500 feet, Lindsay calls *highlands* or *uplands* (Fig. 11).

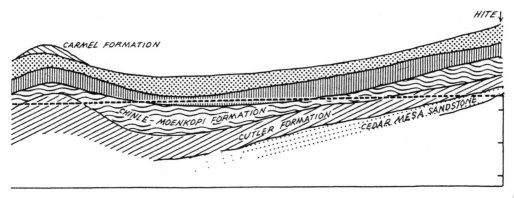

from Cooley, 1958a).

GEOLOGIC TIME				GLEN CANYON STRATIGRAPHY	
ERA	PERIOD	EPOCH	YEARS	STRATIGRAPHIC UNIT	LITHOLOGY AND TOPOGRAPHIC EXPRESSION
Cenozoic	QUATERNARY	RECENT	0 to 63±2 Million	Recent sediments and locally variable formations	
		PLEISTOCENE			
		PLIOCENE			
	TERTIARY	MIOCENE			
		OLIGOCENE			
		EOCENE			
		PALEOCENE			
MESOZOIC	CRETACEOUS		135 ±5 Million	TROPIC SHALE	Dark gray to olive mud stone, thick bedded; seen as rolling, regular and covered slopes; badlands or pediment slopes common.
				DAKOTA SANDSTONE	Grayish buff sandstone, conglomerate and some coal; thick bedded; cross bedded, limonite stained; seen as caprock on cuestas, hogbacks, buttes and mesas
	JURASSIC		180 ±5 Million	MORRISON FORMATION	Generally gray from buff through grayisn red to grayish purple in sandstone, limestone and mudstone; thick to thin bedded; seen as irregular slopes, cliffs and ledges; badlands; caprock on low mesas and cuestas; stripped slopes.
				ENTRADA SANDSTONE	Red buff to white; thick bedded; partly crossbedded; partly flat; seen as rounded and smooth vertical cliffs and irregular ledges; hoodoos.
				CARMEL FORMATION	Deep red siltstone and sandstone; flat, thin to thick bedded; seen as broad and irregular slopes, ledges and caps on low mesas.
				NAVAJO SANDSTONE	Very pale orange and moderate reddish orange; uniform texture; very thick bedded; very large scale crossbedded; 500 to 1500 feet thick; seen as large, vertical, rounded and irregular cliffs, deep canyons, mesas and buttes; alcoves common; widespread stripped surfaces.
	TRIASSIC		230 ±10 Million	KAYENTA FORMATION	Grayish red-purple sandstones; seen as vertical and irregular cliffs and ledges.
				WINGATE SANDSTONE	Reddish brown to pale reddish orange; seen large vertical "columned" cliffs; box canyons.
				CHINLE FORMATION	Light gray through reddish gray and pink to brownish and grayish blue and green sandstone, siltstone and mudstone; seen as irregular slopes, cliffs, ledges.
				MOENKOPI FORMATION	Reddish brown siltstone and sandstone; flat, thin bedded; seen as irregular slopes and ledges.
Paleozoic	PERMIAN		280 ±10 Million	CUTLER FORMATION	Light gray through buff to reddish brown and gray sandstone; seen as irregular ledges and cliffs.
				KAIBAB LIMESTONE	Buff to gray in irregular cliffs.
				RICO FORMATION	Grayish purple cliffs and ledges.
	PENNSYLVANIAN		310	HERMOSA FORMATION	Pinkish gray vert and irreg. cliffs.

Fig. 6. Glen Canyon sediments. (Modified from Zumberge, 1963; Cooley, 1958b; Mullens, 1960).

Although Fig. 10 lists only dominant floral species, the species collected and reported by A. Woodbury, *et al.* (various) run into the hundreds (Clark, 1966). There are differences in the flora between the wide and narrow canyons, with both differing from the flora of the main stem. For example, the towering cottonwood is common in wide side canyons, but rarely grows along the main canyon of the Glen; conversely, Gambel's oak and hackberry are commoner on the main-stem terraces than in the tributaries. While the detailed inventory of all species found in the several ecological niches (A. Woodbury, *et al*, 1959a) need not be repeated here, it is useful to note the range and variety of both floral and faunal species within the area. In one small south bank tributary, Slickrock Canyon (Figs. 2 and 9), which today lacks a perennial stream, 43 families (and nearly 200 species) of plants were collected (Sharrock, *et al.*, 1964). Trees included juniper, willow, oak, elm, hackberry, redbud, ash and salt cedar. Grasses included grama, redtop, cheat, salt, bluestem and many others. Joint fir, rushes, lilies, buckwheat, many chenopods (lamsquarter, etc.), poppets, jimson weed, legumes, cliff rose and serviceberry are among the shrubs and herbs. Composites such as sage, rabbit brush, thistles, sunflower, fleabane and aster also occurred as did cactus and figwort. For better watered canyons the list is even longer.

Mammals and reptiles are numerous, though most are small. In the appropriate vegetation zones, there were such rodents as chipmunk, pocket and other mice, kangaroo rat, woodrats, rabbit, beaver and porcupine. Coyote, red fox, raccoon, ring-tail cat, weasel, badger, river otter (?), spotted skunk and lynx represent the carnivores. Bear and cougar are today transient in the area.

Mule deer, bison and mountain sheep were evidently the only large animals usually found in the entire region; only mule deer now occur in significant number. Toads, salamanders, lizards and snakes were represented widely. The largest of the lizards is the chuckawalla, found commonly in the downstream reaches of Glen. Seven colubrid snakes and two rattler species are common. Because of the variety of habitats (open water, naked sand bars, marsh, river bank vegetation, terraces, hillsides and cliffs and occasional juniper groves), birds are very numerous, ranging from great blue herons and Canadian geese to canyon wrens and hummingbirds.

A few species of small fish—suckers and minnows—are found in the tributaries. Catfish are in the main stem, but few other fish survive there because of the heavy silt load and the turbulence of the sandy bottom,

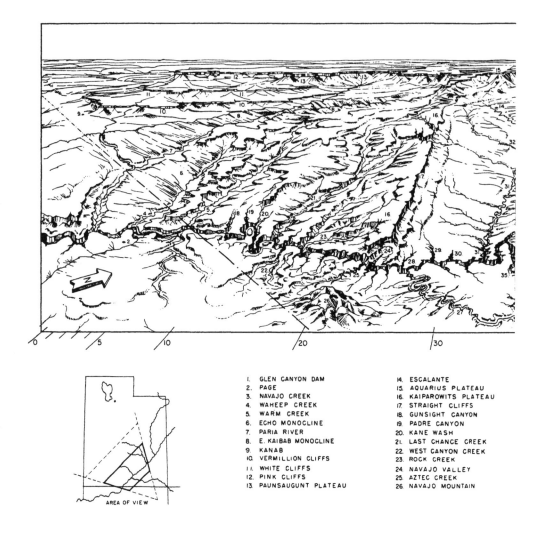

I. GLEN CANYON DAM	14. ESCALANTE
2. PAGE	15. AQUARIUS PLATEAU
3. NAVAJO CREEK	16. KAIPAROWITS PLATEAU
4. WAHEEP CREEK	17. STRAIGHT CLIFFS
5. WARM CREEK	18. GUNSIGHT CANYON
6. ECHO MONOCLINE	19. PADRE CANYON
7. PARIA RIVER	20. KANE WASH
8. E. KAIBAB MONOCLINE	21. LAST CHANCE CREEK
9. KANAB	22. WEST CANYON CREEK
10. VERMILLION CLIFFS	23. ROCK CREEK
11. WHITE CLIFFS	24. NAVAJO VALLEY
12. PINK CLIFFS	25. AZTEC CREEK
13. PAUNSAUGUNT PLATEAU	26. NAVAJO MOUNTAIN

AREA OF VIEW

Fig. 7. Panoramic view of Glen Canyon. (Derived from Hunt, 1956; Ridd, 1963; Lister, 1959a; Raisz, 1946).

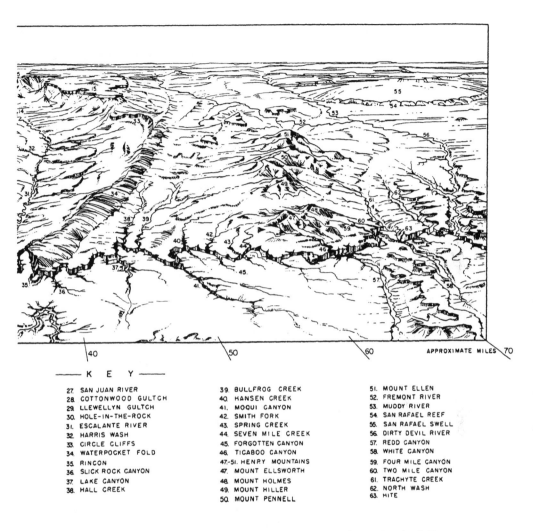

Derived from Hunt, Charles B., 1956 Geological Survey Paper No. 279, *Cenozoic Geology of the Colorado Plateau*, pp. 3, 4, 69; also Ridd, Merrill K., Map supplement no. 3, Annals of the Association of American Geographers, Vol. 53, No. 4, Dec. 1963, *Landforms of Utah in Proportional Relief*; also Lister, Robert H., 1959 U.A.P. No. 39, *Glen Canyon Archeological Survey*, Part I, p.162; also Glen Canyon Archeological Salvage Project, Department of Anthropology, University of Utah and the Center for Western North American Studies, University of Nevada, 1964 map: *Landforms of the Western United States*.

--- K E Y ---

27. SAN JUAN RIVER	39. BULLFROG CREEK	51. MOUNT ELLEN
28. COTTONWOOD GULTCH	40. HANSEN CREEK	52. FREMONT RIVER
29. LLEWELLYN GULTCH	41. MOQUI CANYON	53. MUDDY RIVER
30. HOLE-IN-THE-ROCK	42. SMITH FORK	54. SAN RAFAEL REEF
31. ESCALANTE RIVER	43. SPRING CREEK	55. SAN RAFAEL SWELL
32. HARRIS WASH	44. SEVEN MILE CREEK	56. DIRTY DEVIL RIVER
33. CIRCLE CLIFFS	45. FORGOTTEN CANYON	57. REDD CANYON
34. WATERPOCKET FOLD	46. TICABOO CANYON	58. WHITE CANYON
35. RINCON	47.-51. HENRY MOUNTAINS	59. FOUR MILE CANYON
36. SLICK ROCK CANYON	47. MOUNT ELLSWORTH	60. TWO MILE CANYON
37. LAKE CANYON	48. MOUNT HOLMES	61. TRACHYTE CREEK
38. HALL CREEK	49. MOUNT HILLER	62. NORTH WASH
	50. MOUNT PENNELL	63. HITE

Fig. 8. Examples of Wingate block fracture and Chinle talus covered by spalls in Glen Canyon.

both of which prevent the growth of fish food. A. Woodbury calls the river "an aquatic desert."

To the above assorted species must be added arthropods, as well as parasites and viruses.

Thus, there is the ecological paradox of extreme variety and a score of special and restricted ecological systems merging into a single large system. This comes as a surprise to those who conceive of the desert as barren and lacking in resources.

If all these biotic riches abound, why is the area not more fully exploited by man? The answer lies largely in the quantity and distribution of other than plateau flora. The combined areas for both Glen Canyon and its tributaries of streamside, terrace and hillside vegetation are

Fig. 9. View of Slickrock Canyon, a tributary canyon, showing typical erosional features and vegetation.

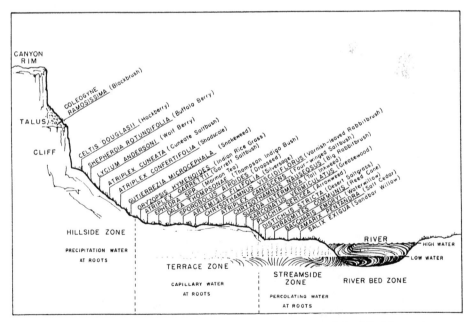

Fig. 10. Zones of floral differentiations in Glen Canyon. (Modified from A. Woodbury, 1965).

Fig. 11. Kaiparowits Plateau, an upland environment with sage flats, pinon and juniper.

reliably estimated at less than 100 square miles, although the Canyon Lands section of the Colorado Plateau contains 150,000 square miles. Moreover, most of the varied fauna are associated with streams—the serpentine ribbons of green which vein the endless expanses of red rock—not with the bare rock and sand plateaus.

It is also true that the biota would respond rather sharply in both extent and richness to lengthy modifications in precipitation pattern. The existence of long and short weather cycles during which actual annual precipitation varies widely are well documented; some of the effects of such fluctuation are well known. Less well understood are the results of what Schoenwetter (in Martin, *et al.*, 1962) has called "environmental shifts"—such as a change in average values based on unchanged physical pattern, or in cases where the precipitation pattern shifts from winter snows to summer rains.

For example, Schulman (1956) documents several centuries of heavier tree ring growth for the Upper Colorado River Basin from approximately A.D. 800 to 1200±. This he interprets as a significant increase in measurable moisture, although Glock (1937; see also Gladwin, n.d.) long before had demonstrated that for yellow pine and other western species the tree ring records only winter moisture, length of growing season, etc.; it says nothing of total annual rainfall. However, I think one can argue that any long series of years with ample winter moisture, as evidenced in a series of broad tree growth rings, can safely be seen as good years characterized by good vegetative growth, strong springs and perennial stream flow. But the converse does not follow; one dare not argue lean or dry years from narrow rings, because the summer rain may have been abundant. Even less, however, can one argue wet summers from lean tree rings alone. An environmental shift toward wet or dry summers must be proved on other grounds—sediments, pollen and the like. We are at present forced to assume several centuries of better ground water conditions from Schulman's findings. Fritt's (1965) work indicates the extreme complexity of determining past climate. His pioneer studies support Glock's views, but season length and average temperatures may be even more important (for tree growth) than precipitation, since the former influences both photosynthesis and food reserves. All in all, no very valuable speculations can be made as to what if any important biotic changes would occur as a result of environmental change.

Although recognized as an agent of erosion and sculptor of land forms, water, as essential to life, is taken entirely for granted where it is plentiful. But in arid regions such as Glen Canyon the distribution of water controls the distribution of living forms; hence, the ecology of the region can almost be reduced to a study of available water and its efficient use. The special and unusual set of circumstances—weather, natural resources and terrain—which characterized the Glen Canyon area have been dwelt upon because it is within this rather rigid environmental frame that any successful exploitation of the region by human beings must be understood.

For the lowlands proper, the picture of attenuated oases set deep within a sandy rocky waste is accurate enough, but for the uplands— the Kaiparowits, Cedar, Cummings, Paiute and other mesas as well as Rainbow Plateau on the flanks of Navajo Mountain—all set back from the river but equally typical parts of the Colorado Plateau—a far less forbidding but poorly watered environment exists. In the lands above 4500–5000 feet in elevation, the pinon and juniper regime dominates. Although surface water is much scarcer, springs and natural reservoirs do exist. Although annual precipitation is greater and summer temperatures are less severe in the uplands than in the canyons, the canyon dweller actually enjoyed the more stable and more plentiful water supply. Ambler, et al. (1964), as well as other authors, emphasize the probable chronic water shortage on the plateaus. Plateau agriculture was thus primarily dry farm; ample evidence of irrigation is reported from the lowlands (e.g., Sharrock, *et al.*, 1961a; Lindsay, 1961a). (See Figs. 27, 28, 29 and 30).

Aside from the less reliable water supplies, the plateaus were the richer zones, judging, of course, by today's conditions. About the same wildlife can be found in both lowlands and uplands but greater numbers are to be found in the uplands. Deer, and their predators, are far more numerous, and rodents too are common. The human occupants of the canyons could, and obviously did, move freely between the differing lowland and upland zones, but the exploitive techniques used by either permanent settlers or transient hunters would differ considerably in detail between the zones. In the larger mesa acreages, for example, choice of hunting range would be uninfluenced by the confining canyon walls. Large game could range more freely, but hunting pressures would likely result less in driving the game away than in imposing a shifting range still within the mesa area, unless the pressure were intense and continuous. The mesa top environment is well exemplified by Cummings Mesa, described by Ambler, *et al.* (1964). Equally illustrative is the high and better watered Kaiparowits briefly sketched by Fowler and Aikens (1963).

In the highlands there are several shrubs, such as mountain mahogany, which were used by the aborigines but which were not found in the canyons. Such materials, however, are found in canyon sites and were presumably easily collected on trips from canyons to the area of occurrence. Thus, as emphasized earlier, for aboriginals the biotic offerings of the Canyon Lands tend to combine several discrete ecological communities into a single larger one extending from river bank to mesa top; all parts of this system were available to and used by the canyon dwellers. Adams, *et al.* (1961) interpret the ecology of the lower Glen in diametrically different terms than here suggested. Because a wide range of species can be collected between the main river course and the outer gorge, they seem to believe that the canyon population stayed close to home, exploiting only the immediate environs. Long (1965), using some of the same data, infers continuous traffic between canyons and mesas; he is even willing to regard the lowland sites as temporary farmsteads visited only in summers by plateau dwellers to the south.

In the crudely drawn ecological context suggested above, no account has been taken of man's effect on the ecosystem, but the nature of man's use of the species in these long narrow strips of associated plants and animals is here the only important point. The rich side canyon oases are far apart, separated by slick rock tablelands covered by dunes and sparse vegetation. Each canyon tends to be an isolated microcosm, with the balance of species within it quite unaffected by other nearby microsystems like it. Separated by the barren stretches of rock, the canyons would each comprise what ecologists call a closed system. Only birds and man, and perhaps other megafauna, could or would move overland, or along the main stem from one tributary to another, and such shift of normal range would be minimal save for man. Seasonal migration by deer or sheep is of course recognized, but within the annual cycle such creatures return to familiar range. Thus, each canyon system is in delicate, and even fragile, balance to the extent that replenishment of species lost through fire, disease or long seasons of adverse climate in any one canyon would be a different and longer process than in situations (such as a mesa or plain) where hundreds or thousands of acres were included in a large continuous tract.

If into these attenuated microcosms man, as hunter of big game, be introduced, the limited game population of each canyon hunted would soon be depleted or dispersed. A hunting band might even move from canyon to canyon but soon the preferred game would be gone and, until it had regenerated or returned from flight, the lands would be unappealing to hunters. If, as is common in America (e.g., O. Stewart, 1956; Swanton, 1928), the cane brakes and thickets were fired to drive out game, the dispersal of game would be more complete, but the period of game regeneration might be quite short in the event of fire hunting, because the fresh new growth that follows a fire quickly attracts a heavier game population. It is important to note that there is widespread occurrence of fine disseminated charcoal or carbonized vegetable matter in buried strata in many of the canyons and on river bars. (See Figs. 12 and 13 for one such extensive charcoal zone on Music Temple Bar.) Similar buried charcoal zones are reported from Moqui Canyon and Castle Wash (Sharrock, *et al.*, 1963) as well as Lake Canyon and other areas (Cooley, 1962). While there is no real certainty that these deposits represent fires, or if they do represent fires, that man set them, the buried carbon bands are quite recent, having just preceded the recent aggradation postulated as having come since A.D. 1, and it is assumed here that if these are widespread fires, they are man's work to be credited to intermittent hunter visits to the canyons, rather than to the later permanent population. If such hunting bands, foraging for both game and vegetable foods in season, were present, both large and small game would be targets as would many plants. Even with only periodic transient predation, however, man's presence could have drastic

Fig. 12. Buried layer of charcoal (dark band) on Music Temple Bar.

effects on the future biota if he introduced to a nonimmunized fauna any of the several diseases for which man is a prime vector (A. Woodbury, 1965).

In situations other than the introduction of disease or in the case of firing, the scant resources would only briefly dwindle, the collecting bands would move on, and man's effect on the ecology would have been negligible. He cannot, in these cases, be seen as a permanent factor in the basic ecosystem. But, should a group establish permanent or continuous residence in any of the canyons, there would result disturbances marked both by the introduction of, and the disappearance of, a few species, with consequent change in the area's nature and desirability as human habitat.

The above statements are far too simple. It is misleading, if not incorrect, to imply that man either does or does not destroy a closed or balanced ecological system. Obviously there are changes in the original balance of the system, but as man becomes part of the system there is a new balance achieved, sometimes one quite deliberately established and preserved by man (Jennings, 1965), by introduction of new species (or disease), even through the use of fire or other "management." To speak of disrupting a specific ecosystem is entirely proper, but the equation is always to be completed by describing the new balance which arises in

Fig. 13. Buried charcoal layer on Music Temple Bar after excavation.

place of the "destroyed" system. The concept of ecological climax and subclimax and the continuous readjustment of species to quite subtle changes in environment, or even in the competitive position of species, is too well documented to debate. The problem here is that archaeological data do not allow subtle evaluation for prehistoric times. The grosser data of archaeology and its supporting disciplines may result in convincing inference, but proof is rarely possible. However, there is good evidence (Yarnell, 1965) that even Pueblo farmers' effect on the land, however slight it may be, is long-lived. He shows from the Bandelier region north of Santa Fe that 21 species appear to be companions of man and are still to be found near Pueblo ruins in the area, having successfully established themselves to survive there for centuries after man's disappearance. Additionally, he gives distributional evidence that several plants (e.g., the Solanaceaes—wild potatoes, tomatoes, etc.) are exotic in this part of the Southwest, and they are presumed actually to have been introduced by the aborigines because of their value as food or for their medicinal or magical properties. What interests human ecologists is not how man "destroys" an ecosystem; our concern is rather what use does man make of a given congeries of species, what species appear (accidentally or deliberately) as a result of man's presence, what is the new balance, how does man manipulate the system to preserve it, and finally how permanently and on what scale does man's activity establish an ecosystem which, after modification, stabilizes during his presence and then restabilizes after his passage. Another consideration here is the density of human population. Sparse occupancy by scattered gardeners would change the natural ecosystem quite differently from the effects of a heavy settlement by similar farmers. Also to be remembered is the fact that wide-ranging collectors of the many wild plants needed by aborigines would have some effect on species many miles from the farming area.

The side canyon communities can probably be thought of as well-balanced ecosystems, even with man intermittently present. But the advent of a permanent population into these surroundings could only succeed through some form of food production. In this case, the pioneer Pueblo brought a gardening technology and the American triad of domesticated food crops, corn, beans and squash. As cultivars, the weeds amaranth, bee-weed and prickly pear can safely be added. In at least two locations—the river bar Benchmark Cave and the upper reaches of Slickrock Canyon—prickly pears were evidently tended and their fruit and pads regularly eaten (Sharrock, et al., 1964) (Figs. 14 and 15). Incidentally, the evidence for quick-fire steaming of cactus pads at Benchmark Cave documents a modern practice as centuries old.

While the way the Pueblo subsistence was divided between the cultigens and cultivars and the native flora is not known, studies convincingly show that a substantial percentage of the number of botanical species found today in the Glen Canyon area has been used by historic tribes as food, medicine and tools. Clark (1966) lists over 920 species reported from the Glen Canyon area and shows that over 390 of these

Fig. 14. Extensive growth of prickly pear, believed to be a food source for Glen Canyon Puebloans.

Fig. 15. Concentrated growth of prickly pear in Slickrock Canyon.

species (not including lichens and mosses) are known from ethnographic accounts to have been used by modern Pueblo tribes. About 110 (28%) of these 390 species have been recovered as part of the archaeological data from the Glen Canyon region. I think it is reasonable, when the modern ethnographic use of a species is established, and its present availability in the Canyon Lands is also certain, to assume the same range of species as subject to similar exploitation in prehistoric times. Recognizing the use of nearly 400 species of native flora by prehistoric Pueblos for food and medicine, to say nothing of those used for tools, weapons, adornment, etc., gives an entirely different perspective on the ecology of the region, especially when it is remembered that to this list of total species exploited, one must add the mammals and birds whose bones/hide/feathers have been recovered in archaeological contexts. It is doubtful that the regular collecting of selected plants would do any particular violence to the balance of the canyon community, after the initial adjustment to man and his introduced species was achieved. The important inference to be made is that the prehistoric peoples did *not* in any sense depend exclusively on their cultivated plants, but incorporated them into their diet and technology as an important, but not the only source of food or raw material. These notions about the utilization of many scores of species are not new. On the contrary they are so generally held as to have been somehow de-emphasized or forgotten, in the face of continuous interest in the "corn, beans and squash" agriculture.

The archaeological debris shows that all large and small mammals and some birds—but rarely fish—were also taken. With respect to aboriginal use of birds, many must have been taken for nondietary reasons. On Rainbow Plateau, Lindsay, *et al.* (1965) report several caches that contained bird skins and feathers, as well as objects decorated with the feathers. Hewes's (1952) classic study of the flicker quill headdress from Mantles Cave argues that, in the one case at least, many birds were taken primarily for their feathers. Save for the larger waterfowl, the food value of the birds represented in the bone and feather collections is slight, and in most cases it seems reasonable to ascribe to them the filling of magical or aesthetic needs rather than dietary ones. The bones of the mountain sheep are the most common, outnumbering deer about seven to one. This scarcity of deer is common over the west (Shutler and Shutler, 1962; Jennings, 1957a). A. Woodbury (1965) thinks the dominance of sheep over deer reflects the preferred habitats of the species, that deer prefer the uplands while sheep range at lower elevations, but the collected evidence is against him, to say nothing of human mobility when in search of game. Durrant (1952) thinks deer were not only less numerous in prehistoric times, but were less widely distributed. In any case, mountain sheep bones are more numerous from *all* archaeological sites in the Glen Canyon area, whether lowland or upland, than are deer. It must be cautioned, however, that distinguishing sheep from deer bones cannot be done with certainty. Only horns, antlers and teeth are indisputable. An unusual variation from the assumed dominance of sheep was recorded from Sand Dune Cave (Lindsay, *et al.*, 1965). The Archaic stratum, estimated at 3000 B.C., yielded many more rabbit bones than sheep. There is no way to tell in this case whether the food bones reflect species availability or food preference. If it is species availability, one is constrained to ask whether the lack of sheep was due to over-hunting, or whether they, as well as the deer, were rare in the Canyon Lands until after the time of Christ. It must also be remembered that while deer and sheep (antelope included) were valuable as food, they also provided raw materials for many artifacts: horn and antler sickles or shredders, punches, flaking tools, spoons and other things; awls of many kinds, dice, gaming pieces and ornaments came from bones; hide was used for leather and cordage, while sinews were used as thread and cordage. Inasmuch as either of the species could provide about the same valuable raw materials of equal quality, the choice of species taken must be a function of some factors other than the use of the various inedible parts. If tradition required that certain classes of tools be derived from one or another particular species, speculations about dietary preference or availability of species becomes irrelevant. What the effect of hunting, with the sheep and deer population becoming lighter as a result of continuing predation by man, may have been upon other species, is hard to assess ecologically. The result might well be an increase in certain plants as browsing and grazing declined. Rodents too might well increase as certain predators—e.g., bobcat—declined in numbers as a consequence of the loss of large animals. Conversely, and equally likely, there would be a decrease in rodent population as carnivores (coyote, fox and bobcat) turned to small animals more intensively. Only experiment could solve such questions.

But hunting and gathering were combined with gardening; the net ecological effect of gardens could not have been drastic. Because of scant water, the tiny garden patches were scattered to take advantage of four or five types of water availability (Hack, 1942; R. Woodbury, 1961) where seepwater, ground water, flash flood diversion, slope runoff or actual diversion of streams provided surface or subsurface irrigation. Although the sandy soil is often rich, its potential is limited to water availability, not fertility. In the canyons, filled with alluvium (Sharrock, *et al.*, 1963), most gardening was probably done on the valley fill itself with ground water being the major source of moisture. Moqui, Navajo and Lake canyons, the largest and most densely populated of the tributaries, testify to this in their coincident distribution of sites and alluvium. Moreover, sites are confined to those reaches of the canyon where the walls are of sandstone and sweet water is available. Where the Chinle forms the bed and banks of the stream, few aboriginal sites are found. The exceptions are Beaver Creek in the San Juan (Lindsay, 1961a), Creeping Dune on the main river (Sharrock, *et al.*, 1961a) (see Figs. 27, 28, 29 and 30), and Loper Ruin at Red Canyon (Lipe, 1960). But in these places, the farming was done on recent sediment, not on Chinle surfaces. The ledges and alcoves of the sandstone also offered preferred habitation and storage sites. Thus, throughout Glen Canyon the distribution of human habitations coincides almost exactly with Navajo, Kayenta and Wingate stream-side outcrops. The Chinle and earlier sediments seldom provided fertile soils. This situation is nowhere better exemplified than in Moqui Canyon (Fig. 16). This coincidence of human use of the geological strata is a phenomenon noted long ago by all students of the Anasazi. The reason for reiterating the point here is to emphasize the probable horticultural reasons, as opposed to an explanation which emphasizes the many natural shelters and caves, overhangs or ledges, as the primary reasons. Apparently the Anasazi built dwelling and storage places where needed; caves and alcoves are merely conveniences, not prerequisites, in the selection of habitation sites. Along the main stem of the Glen, aboriginal use was minor compared to the canyons. A few sites—Loper, Talus, Lizard Alcove—show permanent settlements. Other sites—Smiths Fork and Benchmark Cave—reveal intermittent use over quite a time span, but the overall evidence is that the Glen itself did not attract heavy settlement. No reasonable explanation can be offered for this lack of use. It may be a function of river fluctuation, geology, or even some simple thing like unpalatable drinking water.

Permanent settlement in the canyons should have made several changes in the ecosystem. Aside from the cultigens as new species, with horticulture there would be the first appearance of, or great increase in, the amaranths (and other chenopodia) and bee-weed which thrive in any disturbed soil and especially where there are gardening activities. These plants seem to be ubiquitous associates of corn and squash. Their universal association with corn or with abandoned or fallow fields causes the modern farmer much distress, but they were valued aborigi-

nal foods encouraged by the Pueblo farmer. Evidence from both palynology (Martin and Sharrock, 1964) and ethnohistory indicates that
bee-weed was an important source of food and that the species should
be thought of as a cultigen. Yarnell's (1965) work too would support
the idea of deliberate cultivation of bee-weed as an ancient practice.
The sunflower should probably be considered another deliberately cultivated foodplant.

Another interesting ecological-dietary item gleaned from archaeological evidence is that at site after site in Glen Canyon the corn cobs
showed that the corn had been gathered while still green and the kernels
had been cut off. This implies drying for storage or transport. Cutler
and Bower (1961) speculate that this might mean that frost caught a
late crop, that the farmers were nomadic and harvested when the fields
were visited, or that immature corn was preferred as food. The last al-
ternative seems more tenable; the first two seem to imply a naivete on
the part of the farmers which other evidence of their farming skill
would not support.

There is one artifact which may or may not be a dietary item. At several sites, Lindsay, *et al.* (1965) found many of the "quids" which are
not understood. As a result of experimentation with the common,
sheep-horn sickles they conclude that many quids have not been
chewed at all, but result from the scraping of pulpy flesh and shredding
of the fibers from yucca and other fibrous plants. However, this fails to
account for the masticated-appearing "wads" of mingled fibers (including corn husks, leaves and stalk segments) that are best explained as
having been chewed.

With the carefully tended cultigens and associated "food" weeds
providing the staple foods, the plants of the canyon were exploited sea-
sonally at need. The entire floral complex essentially made up a large
garden. Large animals for food must usually have been rare if one
judges by the paucity of bone compared to other debris at any one site.
(The scantiness of game is, of course, only an inference based on scant
food bone scrap; it rests on no testable finding.) It is reasoned that the
presence of gardeners, who gathered other foods selectively, would
modify somewhat, but by no means disrupt, the canyon ecosystems,
with large animals being the first to feel man's presence and disappear
locally in the face of continuous hunting pressure.

In sum, the human use of the canyons for permanent settlement as-
sumes in response to the special environment a generally uniform distribution in a well defined combination of circumstances. The canyon sites
tend to be confined to the tributaries containing perennial streams, the

36

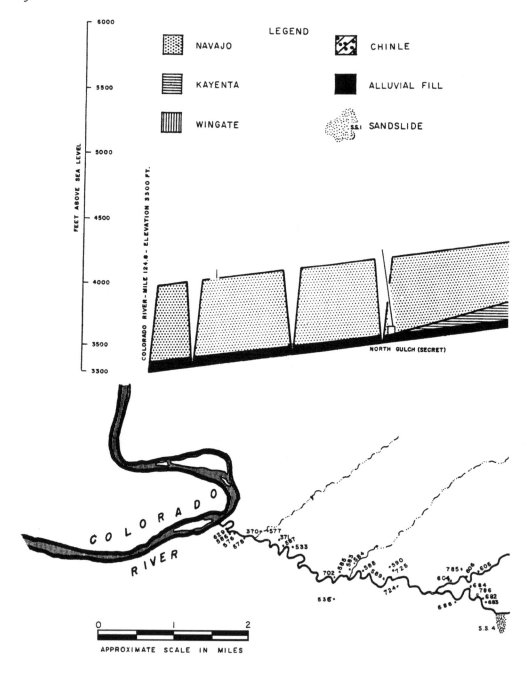

Fig. 16. Relationship of human habitation to geological strata. (Modified from Sharrock, Day and Dibble, 1963).

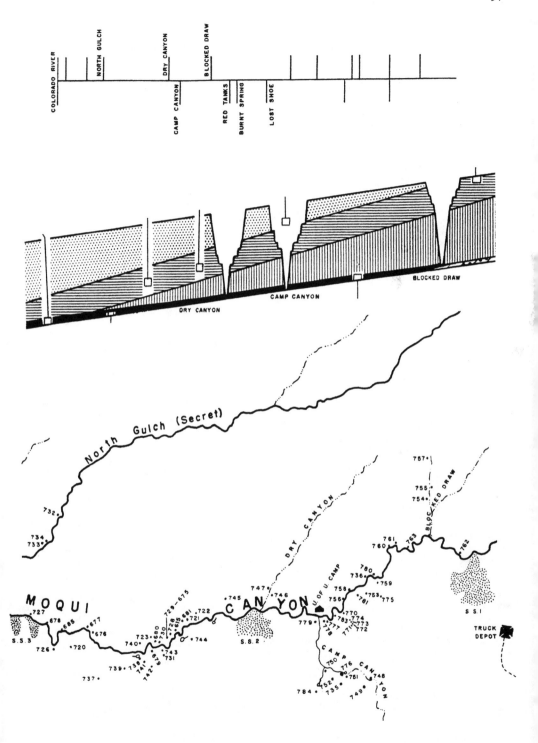

38

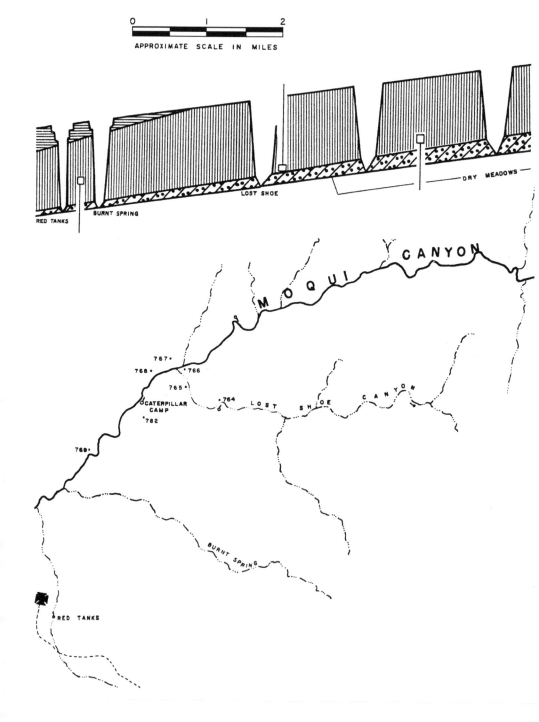

0   1   2
APPROXIMATE SCALE IN MILES

DRY MEADOWS

LOST SHOE

RED TANKS   BURNT SPRING

M O Q U I   C A N Y O N

767·
768·   ·766
765·
·764   L O S T   S H O E   C A N Y O N
○CATERPILLAR
    CAMP
  ·782
769·

BURNT SPRING

■◣
  ○RED TANKS

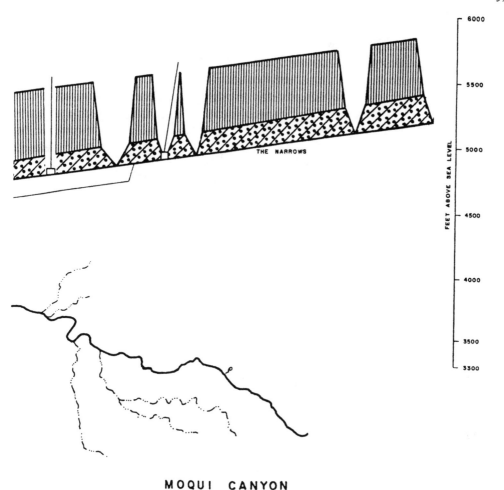

THE NARROWS

FEET ABOVE SEA LEVEL

6000

5500

5000

4500

4000

3500

3300

MOQUI CANYON

SCHEMATIC COMPOSITE OF BOTH BANKS SHOWING
MAJOR GEOLOGICAL FEATURES, TRIBUTARIES AND
DISTRIBUTION OF ARCHEOLOGICAL SITES

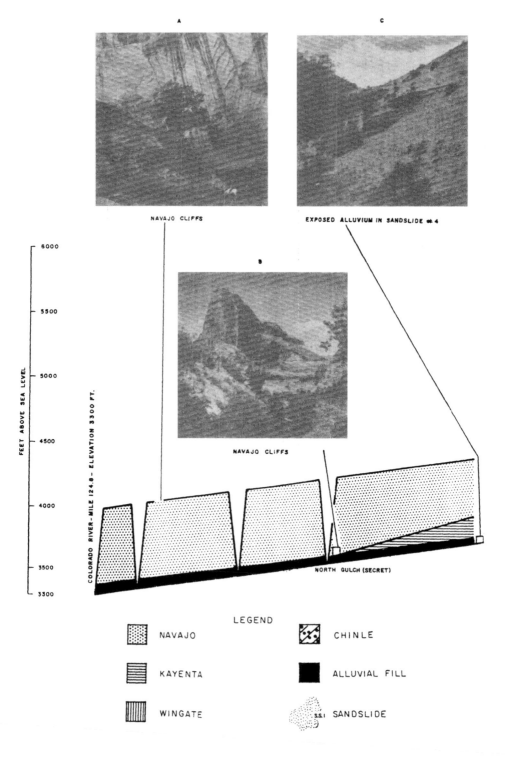

A

NAVAJO CLIFFS

C

EXPOSED ALLUVIUM IN SANDSLIDE at 4

B

NAVAJO CLIFFS

FEET ABOVE SEA LEVEL

COLORADO RIVER—MILE 124.8 — ELEVATION 3300 FT.

NORTH GULCH (SECRET)

6000
5500
5000
4500
4000
3500
3300

LEGEND

NAVAJO

KAYENTA

WINGATE

CHINLE

ALLUVIAL FILL

S.S.I SANDSLIDE

41

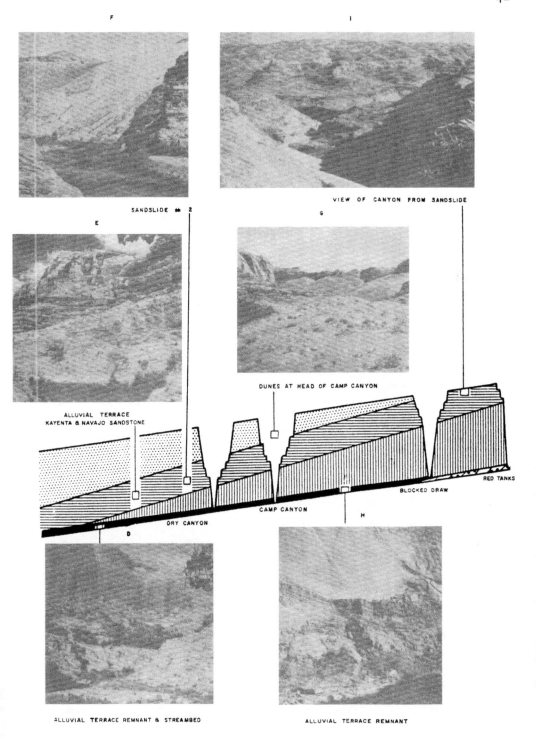

F

I

SANDSLIDE # 2

VIEW OF CANYON FROM SANDSLIDE

E

G

DUNES AT HEAD OF CAMP CANYON

ALLUVIAL TERRACE
KAYENTA & NAVAJO SANDSTONE

RED TANKS

BLOCKED DRAW

CAMP CANYON

DRY CANYON

H

D

ALLUVIAL TERRACE REMNANT & STREAMBED

ALLUVIAL TERRACE REMNANT

K

WINGATE CLIFFS BASED ON CHINLE

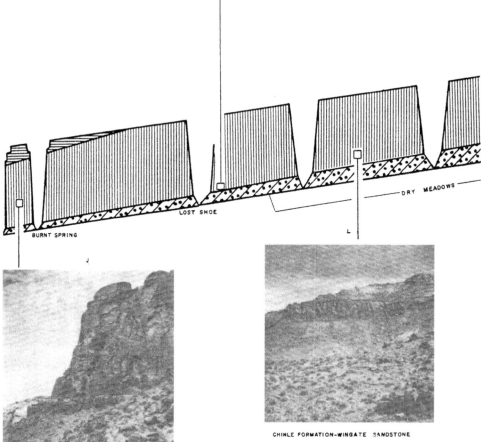

DRY MEADOWS

LOST SHOE

BURNT SPRING

L

J

WINGATE BLOCK FRACTURING

CHINLE FORMATION-WINGATE SANDSTONE
KAYENTA & NAVAJO REMNANTS SET BACK FROM RIM

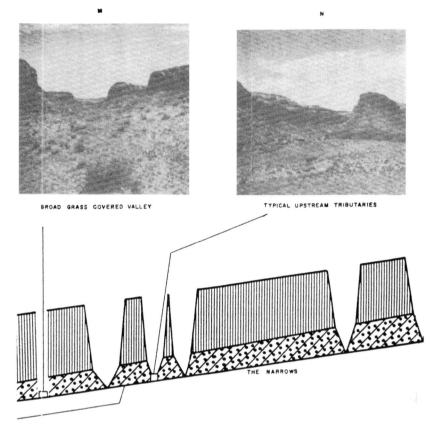

BROAD GRASS COVERED VALLEY

TYPICAL UPSTREAM TRIBUTARIES

THE NARROWS

MOQUI CANYON

SCHEMATIC COMPOSITE OF BOTH BANKS SHOWING MAJOR GEOLOGICAL FEATURES, TRIBUTARIES AND DISTRIBUTION OF ARCHEOLOGICAL SITES

0   1   2

APPROXIMATE SCALE IN MILES

water being derived from springs coming from one or another of the three sandstone members of the Glen Canyon group. When the aboriginals were present, the stream beds contained 25–100 feet of rich alluvium watered by shallow meandering streams, with beaver-meadows and marshes occasionally present (e.g., Lyman Flats and Dead Tree Flats in Lake Canyon [Sharrock, *et al.*, 1961b]). Sites are found only where the sandstone members compose the streamside cliffs, the formations providing the frequently utilized ledges and alcoves. Optimum use was evidently made of scare water, fertile soil and natural species in a satisfactory adjustment or balance extending over three or four centuries.

The same horticultural use of the canyons could *not* be made today because, as mentioned earlier, the original conditions do not now prevail. The sediment is flushed entirely out of the narrower canyons. In the longer, broader canyons the streams flow on bedrock, between remnant pedestals or embankments of valley fill which stand barren and unwatered, with recently dead willow and cottonwood standing upon the old surface attesting the loss of ground water. The gully cutting can be shown to have occurred in Lake Canyon in the twentieth century (Sharrock, *et al.*, 1961b) and probably was not much earlier in the others. As Lance (1963) emphasizes, the canyons have been filled and flushed many times in past millennia; in fact, several sites in Lake and Moqui canyons attest heavy alluviation during occupancy. One site, Red Ant Kiva (Sharrock, *et al.*, 1963), was covered with sediment, and rebuilt three times, with the lowest structures being buried 20 feet below the surface on which dump material from the third building, a Cliff Pueblo above, had fallen. Given the number of sites found on the remnants of fill, the many granaries high in the cliff and the fortunate discovery of Red Ant Kiva (Fig. 17), Lyman Flats and Deadtree Flats in the fill, it is almost a certainty that many more settlements existed in the canyons than have been found. They have been either washed away or covered since abandonment, and were not visible to searchers. It is true that in the highlands the population was evidently denser; at least, the settlements are larger and closer together and there is today an impression of relative plenty and a generally more inviting environment. However, the lowlands were not, in prehistoric times, marginal or undesirable. Being well watered, they were probably more attractive than the uplands, no doubt supporting a population up to full carrying capacity.

While the general rainfall pattern and total precipitation of the lowlands is difficult to infer, two sites gave strong hints of a very wet period sometime *before* the canyons were occupied. This is seen at Davis Kiva

Fig. 17. View of Red Ant Kiva site, remnant of structure eroding out of cutbank.

Fig. 18. View of Glen Canyon a few miles south of the mouth of Red Canyon; Henry Mountains in left background.

46

Fig. 19. View of the University of Utah field crew camp in Moqui Canyon.

(Gunnerson, 1959b), Horseshoe Alcove (Lipe, 1960) and Oakleaf Alcove (Sharrock, *et al.*, 1961b) where there are thick layers of oak leaves, tightly packed, but well preserved, under the current blow-sand surface layer. The Davis Kiva structure pit was dug down through the oak leaves, and the masonry actually laid against the leaves. At Horseshoe Alcove, storage cists were dug through a similar layer. In each location, a few oak trees still survive and many dead snags bespeak a stronger stand recently. But no such blanket of leaves now accumulates. Hence, it is reasoned that these same overhangs, in wetter times, once sheltered larger groves of oak and that there was no decay of the fallen leaves because of the shelter. These observations do not help any with understanding the human ecology, unless heavy acorn crops might have helped attract some of the scattered archaic peoples into the area, be-

Fig. 20. Glen Canyon area scene: Lobo Arch in Coyote Gulch.

cause the deposit seems to antedate slightly all apparent human use of the lowlands. It is interesting to note that a similar litter of oak leaves was reported at DuPont Cave, near Kanab, Utah, deposited at some time earlier than Basketmaker II use of the cave (Nusbaum, 1922).

While the Canyon Lands may seem dangerous and difficult to moderns, they presented little threat to mobile aboriginals with special exploitive skills and intimate knowledge of the terrain and its resources. The main stem of the Glen can be entered from most of the side canyons, and at a score of points the ancient hand and toe trails up the cliffs mark points of easy descent/ascent between streamside and plateau rim (Adams, et al., 1961; Ambler, et al., 1964; Long, 1965) (see Figs. 31, 32, and 33). The river itself could be easily crossed in many places all year round (except during flood stage in the late spring and

Fig. 21. View of Kaiparowits Plateau from Hole-in-the-Rock.

early summer) by fording or by swimming a few strokes. Because wheeled vehicles have been able to cross in only a few spots the Canyon Lands have loomed in recent years as a barrier to communication, but to horsemen (using the Ute Trail near Padre Creek, for example) or people on foot, the river was less a barrier than a brief inconvenience. Crossing of the San Juan River was equally easy. At Paiute Farms and Wilson Canyon well known trails crossed; the latter trail was a trade route used by Hopi, Paiute, Navajo and whites.

The purpose of this chapter is to suggest that the canyons and the uplands were aboriginally a single ecosystem and that the aboriginal occupants of the area exploited the resources on this basis. There are also data on the reasons for abandonment—i.e., environmental change. These data tend to support the conclusions of Schoenwetter (1962; Schoenwetter, *et al.*, 1964) and others, from other sectors of the Anasazi province. Equally important is the reminder from the canyons of the broad spectrum of species used by the Pueblo for centuries in conjunction with the famous triad of cultigens. While the role of corn, beans and squash was probably crucial in providing the difference in survival year after year, survival would have not been possible with these alone. The reliance of the gardener upon wild foods is not a new concept. It is merely an oft-forgotten one, here reinforced.

Fig. 22. View of Fence Ruin site 100–150 ft. above stream bed in Wilson Canyon. Member of University of Utah excavation crew descending from site by means of a rope.

Most valuable is a changed perspective on the genius of Pueblo culture. The intricate trail system, the exploitation of scores of plants, animals and minerals, the skill with which scarce water was utilized and the several centuries of use the data show all serve to remind that, in a sense, *all* Pueblo are exploiters of marginal land, marginal, that is, so far as agriculture is concerned. And that their persistence/survival into

modern times bespeaks traditional foraging techniques rarely mentioned in the descriptions of the Pueblo lifeway. Elsewhere (Jennings,
1963b) I have characterized the Pueblo genius:

> ... If the Pueblo can be seen as subsistence gardeners representing a cul-
> ture whose limits were closely geared to some minimal rainfall line, if
> we can see the Pueblo as expanding and contracting territorially in al-
> most annual response to climatic/rainfall conditions, if we can see theirs
> as a lifeway viable beyond anything we know now, then perhaps we can
> understand its details and its survival. If we can see beyond the neat suc-
> cession of visible variations in the areas of dense population, we can see
> that the religious richness, the compulsive artistry and the overwhelm-
> ing architecture are typical only where they occur. The typical Anasazi
> were clever, ingenious small farmers whose ability to exploit the envi-
> ronment was equal to, and possibly derived from, the desert culture an-
> cestor whose skills were retained in large degree ...

Given the setting, and an ecological bias in interpretation of the
setting as a background, we turn now to the prehistory of the Glen
Canyon area and the contributions of the Glen Canyon research.

Glen Canyon Chronology

Lithic–Archaic–Formative

The sequence of cultural succession in the Southwest, as now understood, can be best appreciated as part of the larger prehistory of North America. Habitation of the western hemisphere by man cannot be demonstrated as any earlier than 10,000 B.C., although on logical or sentimental grounds some scholars would establish 30,000 B.C. or even 40,000 B.C. as the probable date of first occupancy. A generally used series of sequent or coexistent cultural stages for the New World devised by Willey and Phillips (1958) labels the earliest cultures known as the Lithic, followed uniformly over the continent by the Archaic, with the latter transforming into a Formative stage in some areas. Out of the Formative the Classic stage evolves in an even more restricted zone in Central America. The Lithic stage is usually characterized as being focused on big-game hunting to the near exclusion of other subsistence sources. In the western United States the artifacts ascribed to this stage are crude and roughly formed. Elsewhere excellent well chipped points, gravers, prismatic knives and several scraper forms are the usual complex. There is next a transition into a widespread Archaic wherein a score of discrete local artifact congeries are lumped in a stage characterized by a wide range of special gathering tools which bespeak a subsistence base aimed at wide, if not complete, exploitation of available plant and animal species. Thus, the Lithic is described as having a uni-based subsistence with the Archaic being multi-based. The distinction is quite useful, being that of the specialist hunter vs. the forager who has many exploitive skills. The Formative, by definition, involves a more complex technology based on horticulture—a food-producing stage in contrast to the preceding collecting and gathering stages.

These three stages—Lithic, Archaic, Formative—are all documented for the West, where the Lithic is not yet fully understood but the Archaic, often called the Desert Archaic or Desert Culture, is well represented and in some degree assessed. The Desert Culture, as the name implies, may as some claim, reflect a lifeway and a constellation of artifacts peculiarly adapted to the desert and its scant biota. Whether this apparent restriction makes sense is here irrelevant; the Desert Culture clearly bespeaks the Archaic stage. The generalized attributes of the Desert Culture as first described (Jennings, 1956) occur from the Rockies to the West Coast, and from the Canadian border to the Valley of Mexico, thus embracing the Southwest. The simple technology, though special, is adapted to constant wandering over a yearly round from one seasonal vegetable food source to another. The key artifacts are the flat slab milling stone and a variety of baskets and textiles but there are a host of other diagnostic artifact forms. Several of these Desert Archaic assemblages within the Southwest are described and named; in eastern Utah and western Colorado the Uncompahgre (Wormington and Lister, 1956) has been described; for southern Arizona and southwestern New Mexico the Cochise sequence was reported by Sayles and Antevs (1941); the Concho or north central Arizona and the Lobo in western New Mexico all exemplify the Archaic stage.

Wherever it is studied, the Archaic pattern of exploitation is about the same, bespeaking skill and ingenuity in exploiting a spectrum of plants not recognized by moderns as edible or otherwise useful to humans. The universally distributed Desert Archaic stage is recognized as the base out of which the Southwestern Formative stage emerged. The emergence resulted from the acceptance of traits diffusing northward out of Mexico. The new traits were horticulture involving the three major food crops (as well as some edible plants now regarded as weeds), the idea of pottery and possibly pit house architecture, followed by stone masonry. All these occur earlier in Mexico (MacNeish, 1964) than they appear to have existed in North America. There is evidence, the significance of which is not yet well understood, that primitive maize had been introduced into the Southwest at Bat Cave, New Mexico, by about 3000 B.C., but this stands as an isolated occurrence. Significant production of corn cannot be proved until about 1000 B.C.; the evidence is from Tularosa Cave, New Mexico (Martin, et al., 1952). Pottery was introduced by 300 B.C. according to Martin, et al. (1952), but Bullard (1962) strongly implies that this conclusion rests on erroneous data. Hence, while the timing may still be obscure, there is agreement that by the time of Christ there existed in southwestern New Mexico a new and simple culture based on plant cultivation, possessing good pottery, with loosely knit permanent villages of pit houses. This manifestation, now known as Mogollon, is the earliest of the Pueblo cultures and is assigned an ancestral role. That it preserves much of the technology of the earlier Archaic is attested by scores of artifact classes and in details of technology. There is increasing and convincing evidence that the spread of the relatively simple Mogollon pattern, which evolved from the slow adoption of the new traits by a Desert Archaic stage population, remained unmodified over most of the Southwest as far north as the Colorado River and into the Four-Corners area long before A.D. 500. This spread is marked by a brown pottery tradition, the pit house with certain distinctive features and other traits. By A.D. 500, however, the northern provinces had begun to develop distinctive technological and architectural traits. This younger constellation is called Anasazi Pueblo as distinguished from the Western Pueblo or Mogollon. What has come to be called Anasazi appears to result from a blend of traits diffused northward from the Mogollon center to a resident Archaic population at about A.D. 1. The earliest Anasazi pottery is in the southern/western brownware tradition; the dwellings are sometimes in pits but also occur above ground. The Little Colorado River is usually thought of as the boundary between the Western and the Anasazi zones of dominance.

Consideration of Glen Canyon, of course, restricts us to the Anasazi district, the largest of the Pueblo provinces. Usually included within the Anasazi are the Mesa Verde, Chaco, de Chelly, Kayenta-Virgin and Fremont–Sevier-Fremont sub areas. All of these local variants impinge upon the Glen Canyon area. The emergence of the Anasazi from the Desert Archaic seems to have been in response to Mexican influences via Mogollon, but additional contacts can be seen, and the end product or climax about A.D. 1300 was quite different from contemporary Mogollon. The Mesa Verde Anasazi may well have been strongly affected by Formative influence from the south and southeast in such things as pottery shapes and decorative techniques (Phillips, *et al.*, 1951; Jennings, 1956), but clarification of this point awaits more study.

Anasazi Classification

Although the sequence of cultural development for the Anasazi has been reasonably well known since about 1920, it was formalized by the 1927 Pecos Classification. The Pecos scheme recognized the change in complexity and technology of the inhabitants of the Four-Corners area over a long period of time, beginning with a simple, nonceramic Archaic culture and extending to the modern Pueblo Indians. The effects, good and ill, of this classification upon thought and increased understanding of southwest prehistory have been assessed time after time (Roberts, 1935; Brew, 1946; W. Taylor, 1948; Bullard, 1962, are among the most perceptive). Generally the effect of the classification has been deleterious because the original highly tentative suggestions hardened almost overnight into eternal verity and were used as a rigid standard of measurement instead of as the flexible guide to study that the authors had hoped to establish.

The sequence took account of eight sequent stages, Basketmaker I, II, III, Pueblo I, II, III, IV, and V. Each, except Basketmaker I, was characterized by artifacts and culture practices which were quite explicitly listed. Eventually, with the aid of dendrochronology, it was possible to bracket these successive stages rather closely in time, so the stages came also to be periods of time. Many useful modifications of these terms have been devised (Roberts, 1937; Daifuku, 1952, 1961; McGregor, 1965) but the original periods are dominant in the literature. Basketmaker I was then hypothesized because, although logically necessary, it had not been recognized archaeologically. Long since, the Desert Archaic stratum has provided cultural substratum implied by the Basketmaker I stage of Daifuku.

Today, the Anasazi stages are usually assigned about these dates:

Basketmaker I = Pre A.D. 1
Basketmaker II = A.D. 1–500
Basketmaker III = A.D. 450–750
Pueblo I (where encountered) = 750–900
Pueblo II = 850–1100
Pueblo III = 1100–1300
Pueblo IV = 1300–1700
Pueblo V = 1700 to present

While these neat 200 year divisions may appear almost arbitrary, they are supported by much data. These periods, however, are not of the same length nor do they cover the same time spans over the entire Southwest. For example, in the area south of the Colorado River, Lindsay, et al. (1965) offer a modified chronology as follows:

Desert Culture tradition = Pre A.D. 1
Basketmaker II = Pre A.D. 1–600 (700 in some areas)
Basketmaker III = A.D. 600–800
Pueblo I = A.D. 800–1000
Pueblo II = A.D. 1000–1150
Pueblo III = A.D. 1150–1300
Pueblo IV = 1300–1850
Pueblo V = 1850 to present

Daifuku (1952, 1961) in a broader scheme, more useful for some purposes, has a different terminology and greater time spans as follows:

Elementary = Pre A.D. 1
Basic = A.D. 1–700
Florescent = 700–1300
Fusion = 1300–1600

A defect in the original scheme is the nebulous character of Pueblo I and its limited distribution. Reed (1963b), in an attempt to clarify the significance of the Pueblo I stage, documents the imprecision or at least their nonexclusive occurrence of the traits ascribed to Pueblo I. Failure to find a Pueblo I period, in his words only means the "absence or scarcity of banded necks on the gray ware and of Kana-a style on the black-and-white." However, the sequent stages do not demonstrate clean-cut differences so sharp as to justify a beginning and end to every stage by any given year. The stages, over the Anasazi area, have certain reality but the blending or transition of one stage into another, the rapid developments in one area and the equally characteristic lag in following innovation in another area leave the dated periods almost useless if a period ascription is meant to represent *both* 1) a stage or the traits represented (i.e., content of a site or area) by stage and 2) time span. This being true, the Basketmaker-Pueblo series has come increasingly to carry time as the major connotation.

As indicators of time, major reliance has been placed by most scholars on distinctive ceramic wares. These wares are broken into numerous types, types which seem to have either a restricted geographic range, or were limited to a few years' (or centuries') span of manufacture and use. Such index types have been very useful, providing clues to age not inferable from any other of the arts and crafts, which seem to be maddeningly complacent (R. Woodbury, 1954). Ceramic type usefulness in telling time has much diminished as research has shown that many types were manufactured over a much longer timespan than was originally credited to them. (Breternitz, 1963; Ambler, *et al.*, 1964; Lindsay, *et al.*, 1965; Sharrock, *et al.*, 1961b).

Occupational Patterns and Timespans

As for the Glen Canyon itself, occupancy was, as has been implied, not continuous nor equally heavy throughout the area. For one thing, not all parts of the area were equally attractive. Of the many tributaries (see Fig. 2) Moqui, Navajo and Lake canyons show the longest, as well as the heaviest use in the Canyon Lands. An exception is the Escalante River–Boulder Creek system. In fact, the Escalante system is a special case, almost duplicating in miniature the Glen Canyon. The Escalante is a long perennial stream, fed by long right bank tributaries containing numerous aboriginal sites in the areas of broad alluvial flats and perennial or seasonal streams. Its left bank tributaries are shorter and less frequently contain streams and aboriginal sites are rare.

Away from the canyons the heavy occupancy of Boulder Creek Valley (Lister, various; Gunnerson, 1959b) as well as the dense settlement of the Kaiparowits Plateau (Gunnerson, 1959a; Fowler and Aikens, 1963), falls late in the occupation sequence, and is probably best explained by the greater resources of the higher elevation (up to 7200 ft.), i.e., richer biota, better soils, and apparently heavier precipitation. In the same way plateaus south of the Glen—Paiute and Cummings mesas, and Rainbow Plateau—were probably more desirable for the same set of favorable environmental reasons (Ambler, et al., 1964).

If one considers the full area one does find the entire chronological sweep of the Anasazi occupancy represented, but the distribution is spotty and discontinuous until Pueblo II and III times. No evidence of the big game hunters of 5000–8000 B.C. was discovered. The Desert Archaic (Daifuku's Elementary stage) is probably represented by the several nonceramic sites, but none yielded diagnostic artifacts. Nonetheless Lindsay, et al. (1965), Long (1965), Lipe, et al. (1960), and Sharrock, et al. (1963, 1964) found and assigned nonceramic sites on the main stem, on most of the tributaries and in Castle Wash to a pre-Basketmaker III stage. Nearly all sites so assigned were buried and the preceramic ascription is probably correct. The use of the sites would appear to at least precede the Tsegi period of aggradation with which the Pueblo II sites are associated.

In Castle Wash, two nonceramic sites were dug and more noted. These are all assigned to the Basketmaker stage but more on faith than evidence. Later, the Lone Tree Dune site (42Sa–363) (Sharrock, et al., 1963) was C–14 dated at A.D. 250±80, a date consistent with the Basketmaker II assemblage of artifacts at the site. In the canyons, it is in Moqui Canyon that the best documented Basketmaker occupancy occurs. Here, there were sites rich enough to attract three expeditions from 1897 to 1929 (Adams, 1960; Sharrock, et al., 1963). In 1961, excavation of the leavings from earlier Bernheimer Expeditions yielded a good and varied collection of materials ascribed, typologically, to the Basketmaker II stage, presumed, of course, to have been derived (migrant) from the Basketmaker center to the east. One Basketmaker II site was noted in Oak Canyon. On Cedar Mesa numerous Basketmaker sites are rumored to exist. One excavated site (42Sa313) (Sharrock, *et al.*, 1964) on Cedar Mesa is interpreted as late Basketmaker III.

The Moqui Canyon sites—Rehab Center and Bernheimer Alcove—were stratified with Pueblo remains over, and mixed with, the Basketmaker type containing mummified bodies with no cranial deformation (Reed, 1963a). Artifacts associated with the burials were scant but of diagnostic kinds of basketry, yucca cloth and flexible bags, but there was no pottery. No heavy deposits of midden or debris were apparent anywhere, so this first infiltration is presumed to have been of short duration. With the departure of this early population, the entire area seems to have been without permanent occupancy.

Basketmaker III is not represented in any canyon except Navajo where it is reported from a tributary. Pueblo I is claimed for Navajo Canyon on the lower Glen (Long, 1965). It was only in Pubelo II times that heavy settlement of the lowland canyon system is reported. This time it was more general and complete. Although some canyons were not continuously occupied, some were used until late Pueblo III.

On the plateaus, about the same pattern can be charted archaeologically except that one cave—Sand Dune—shows strong Basketmaker use, and an earlier Desert Archaic deposit dated at perhaps 3000 B.C. was also reported. Occupancy seems to have continued until the abandonment of the northern Anasazi regions in the later thirteenth century.

Cultural Lines of Communications

As Glen Canyon research progressed, authors tended more and more to speak of the canyon dwellers as being an overflow population pushed into a marginal environment. While this view is defensible, it is at best only a partial explanation of the distribution of the settlements. In fact, the evidence is that, far from being marginal, the canyons were desired spots, with the uplands—Cummings Mesa, Boulder and Escalante valleys, Kaiparowits Plateau—being occupied later than the lowlands in the face of improved climate and possible population increase. The Mesa Verde influences in the canyon system are confined to the Colorado and its east bank tributaries, largely upstream from Moqui Canyon. The remains in the lower part of the triangle and the lower Glen Canyon downstream from Moqui Canyon are heavily Kayentan. Moreover, the Kayenta appear to have made two upstream thrusts, one about A.D. 900 and the other, more extensive, *ca.* A.D. 1100

(Lipe, *et al.*, 1960). Also, the Kayenta crossed the Glen Canyon and followed up the Escalante River and Boulder Creek to establish a long communication line, and a large, distant outpost deep in Fremont country (Lister, various). They also dominated the Kaiparowits. The ceramic and architectural evidence is that the Kayenta and Fremont populations blended, or were in intimate contact, at the Coombs site. All this looks less like marginality than like aggressive colonization by Kayentans, a process somehow different from casual, unorganized drift of excess population into the nearby canyons where the potential for agriculture existed, but limited in both arable acreage and water resources. At Point of Pines (Haury, 1958), there is a later evidence of Kayenta colonization (at both Coombs and Point of Pines, the Kayenta villages were destroyed by fire during occupancy). To ascribe the spread of traits of Kayenta origin to any specific colonial plan is probably ridiculous, but it must be remarked that Kayenta-inspired ceramic traits, at least, extend far west and north of the heartland along the left bank of the Glen Canyon stretch of river. Whatever the explanation, the Kayentans were clearly a viable and widespread people with extensive contacts after A.D. 1100.

Although the canyon complex is the focus of our concern, it can be understood as having no unique cultural contribution of its own; its history reflects what went on in the highlands to the north and south, and is readily fitted into the broader frame of Southwestern prehistory.

The Glen can be thought of as no great barrier to communications but it actually does appear to serve as an often crossed boundary between several named cultural subprovinces of the Southwest (see Fig. 23). To the south lies the Kayenta Anasazi group, to the east, Mesa Verde Anasazi, and touching the river on the north is the Fremont culture which covers eastern Utah but is not very well understood in its relationships to the Anasazi (see Aikens, 1966a). West of the Glen, and north of the Colorado, is the Virgin area, which can be included with Kayenta (Aikens, 1966b). All these "branches," as they are sometimes called, are local variants of the Pueblo tradition that is recognized over parts of four states, having achieved a maximum distribution before A.D. 1300. They are still extant in remnant form in the modern towns of the Rio Grande and the western Pueblo towns.

The several branches show marked differences in minor crafts and variations in locale and population density but these local differences should not obscure, for the student, the great uniformity of the Anasazi subcultures. All are characterized by small scattered settlements, with the larger settlements apparently being little more than aggregations or

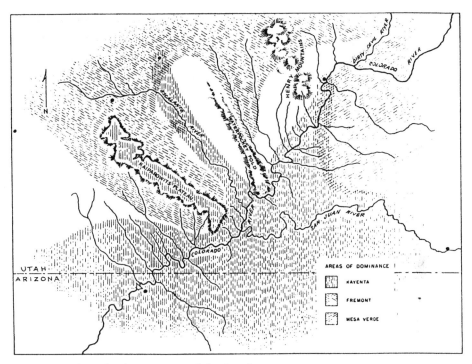

Fig. 23. Cultural subprovinces of the Southwest.

clusters of several small units. In these later situations the small units, in their separation from one another, effectively preserve the earlier scattered settlement pattern. (See especially the Kayenta in Lindsay, *et al.*, 1965). All depend primarily on a mixed gardening and collecting subsistence, with the hardy annuals, beans, corn and squash, providing part of the diet. Cotton is common also in the later time periods; empty bolls and carefully preserved caches of seed probably imply that cotton was raised locally. All Anasazi show great technological skill in utilizing available materials for tools, utensils, ornaments, and clothing. In particular, ceramics of good technical quality and usually great artistic merit characterize all the area. No evidence of concerted political or military action exists; archaeological evidence, buttressed by ethnologic data, suggests the autonomy of every little settlement, with confederation or union only seen in the face of some grave shared threat. The Pueblo uprising in the seventeenth century might exemplify united action in stress situations. There seems little doubt that communication and exchange of ideas was extensive and continuous over the Southwest for most of Pueblo dominance (Reed, 1964b).

By almost any geographic standard, other than European, the area where Pueblo remains are common is very small. Portions of only four states are involved. Few readers will realize how small the entire Southwest is or that Glen Canyon Dam lies about in the center of the area where Southwestern cultures are represented. Using the dam as a center, a 300-mile radius describes a circle which includes Ogden, Utah, Las Vegas, Nevada, Phoenix and Tucson, Arizona, Reserve, Albuquerque and Santa Fe, New Mexico, and Alamosa and Artesia, Colorado. Placing Glen Canyon Dam at the center of the Pueblo area has no validity except as doing so succeeds in showing something that is more important. The dam lies only 269.5 air miles from the western Pueblo area and 171.5 miles from Mesa Verde. The headwater of Lake Powell at Hite is only 69.6 miles from the Fruita-Emery axis where the Fremont culture dominates. The Colorado River, for most of its length, is believed to separate the "real" Pueblo area from the "peripheral" northern half of the imaginary circle, although the expansion to the north is believed to have occurred during Pueblo II times or is at least thus credited by most authors.

Contributions of the
Glen Canyon Research

Assessment

Glen Canyon studies in archaeology were handicapped at the outset because well controlled data defining the several areas were not available. In a real sense, the Glen Canyon findings stood in an informational vacuum with chronological controls insecure and no definitive descriptions (even of Kayenta) then available for consultation. This situation left the need to develop comparative material outside Glen Canyon in order to better understand the latter collections. With other funds, concurrent with Glen Canyon project work proper, excavations were undertaken at the Coombs site, Boulder, Utah (Lister, various), on the Kaiparowits Plateau, in the vicinity of St. George, Utah, in Zion National Park and in Johnson Canyon east of Kanab, Utah. Thus, the chain of new data north of the Colorado, extends from the Glen Canyon westward to the heart of the Virgin Branch area. These findings when coupled with the reports by Schroeder (1955) and Shutler (1961) reporting work done in the 1930's by other investigators, will clarify the Virgin branch (Aikens, 1966b). To the north, the heavily Kayentan Coombs site documents, as does Harris Wash (Fowler, 1963) and other evidence (F. Lister, 1964), intimate contact with the Fremont area. To the east, the situation is clearer as to the strong Mesa Verde connections of southeastern Utah remains. To the south, the Museum of Northern Arizona studies in the Kayenta Branch, simultaneous with those of Utah, now provide a solid corpus of comparative and control material, but these data were not available until the Glen Canyon project was completed.

As for Glen Canyon, Adams (1960) has shown that the region has been tramped over by archaeologists for a century; they, however, left home with their objectives already set. Most were searching, not for whatever they might find, but for a replication of what had already been found elsewhere. Southwest archaeology has its roots in the romantic urges of a few scholars and in the collector/explorer/adventurer set.

The formal study of the prehistory of Glen Canyon began, of course, with Major Powell in 1869 when he discovered and described the Loper Ruin (Lipe, 1960) at the mouth of Red Canyon. Subsequently, as shown by Adams (1960), no less than *thirty-seven* major expeditions had, by 1957, ventured into the canyon with archaeological research as their professed aim. Even so, it was possible to refer correctly to the entire area as archaeologically *terra incognita* (Adams, 1960). Had any of the army of investigators been better equipped or better informed or stayed longer or aimed at providing a record or mounted a systematic attack, the entire Glen Canyon salvage project would have been unnecessary. What the early searchers found entered into the vast body of unwritten lore of Southwest archaeology and thus never served science particularly well. The ravages committed by these men left the students of the middle twentieth century "picking over the leavings of countless predecessors" (Adams, 1960).

While it is possible to be highly critical of the early explorers, to do so would reveal the critic to be not only unfair but uninformed. The Glen Canyon complex of slickrock and canyon has held a romantic appeal since its discovery. The major and many of the minor expeditions were searchers, not researchers (Crampton, various; Adams, 1960). Archaeology, for the early visitors, was as much a justification as an objective. What this small army of men wanted was excitement, the thrill of seeing empty and deserted lands and the compelling omnipresent possibility of finding some new eighth Western wonder. To judge them as archaeologists is, in a sense, to misunderstand them and their times.

Even the failure of the illustrious frontrunners to report, however, is a function of time and circumstance and fashion. If one is not a trained anthropologist, yet holds forever in his mind memories and visions of Mesa Verde's fabled artifactual riches, and confidently hopes to find other towering castles containing comparable artistic wealth, the mouldering ruins of a small granary or a thin camp site where a few sherds remain in evidence, would not be deemed worthy of meticulous reporting. In a measure then, and in the breach, the Glen Canyon *had* been observed, adjudged by "experts" and assessed as negligible, meriting neither study nor review. Even when some explorer actually prepared a report, perhaps preliminary in coverage, or put his notes or diary on file (Adams, 1960), authority ruled against or otherwise failed to publish. Or equally probable, the explorers' interest flagged in the face of non-spectacularity and so the preliminary report remained the only one. But the fact remains that no one person or program worked systematically to learn the region. All seemed to be in haste, probably in haste because logistic problems once put all canyon explorers on rationed time. All, failing to find the hoped-for richness, nonetheless perpetuated the tales told by lonely cowhands and miners as to the vast ruins and rich artifact contents in "other canyons" or distant plateaus (e.g., Steward, 1941).

For whatever the complex of reasons and despite the involvement of such eminent men as Morris, Cummings, Judd, J. Wetherill, Morss, Beals, Brainerd, Kluckhon, and Steward, when the threat of Lake Powell came, scientists were unable to certify that the region was sufficiently known. Hence, the salvage operation being reported here was necessary.

Expectations and Results

At the outset of the salvage work, the field operations were expected to yield evidence of at least three major periods of occupancy of the Glen Canyon Region: Earliest, it was thought would be significant evidence of some local version of western Archaic culture—such as the fabled Basketmaker I or the Uncompahgre or some unnamed variant. This stage would have fallen chronologically to the millennia before Christ. Then, confidently, it was assumed that the full range of Anasazi from Basketmaker II to Pueblo III would be isolated, in stratigraphic sequence, at site after site on the main stem and in many a canyon. Finally, after abandonment of the region by Anasazi, the scattered camps of proto-historic and historic Indians—Hopi and Navajo to the south and Shoshone speaking Ute and Paiute to the north—were to have been identified. No such sequence was found to exist, or at least it cannot be thoroughly documented.

The reduction of expectation does not invalidate the original scope, nor does it diminish the value of the actual findings. While the actual results seem at times to have been redundant and field work seems perhaps to have been carried to the point of diminishing returns, there are here two considerations of relevance. First, it can be pointed out that science does not suffer from, but insists upon, repeated occurrences. And, second, stable certain knowledge or data rooted in systematic continuous investigation and the collection of masses of supporting data is infinitely more useful to science than comparable or identical ideas developed through inference from lesser or inadequate sampling.

As to the increments to the broad field of general knowledge accruing from the program, the major fields affected include ecology, history, ethnology and prehistory. Data gathered and made available through publication in these fields are probably more numerous than for any area of equal size in the West. This collecting and reporting can in itself be supposed to be a contribution because within the vast corpus of varied data, reported only in descriptive form, there are certainly answers to yet unasked questions. For example, a question that could be asked eventually is why kivas were fouled or desecrated by placing human fecal matter in the fireplaces. Gunnerson reports this phenomenon at Davis Kiva as does Lipe at Talus Ruin. Perhaps through fastidiousness on the part of the authors, neither find was mentioned in the technical reports, but they were mentioned in the field notes. In addition, at Steer Palace (Sharrock, *et al.*, 1964) an aged female was buried by being crammed into the fireplace of a classic kiva. Even disregarding any future gains in knowledge students may derive, the data can be judged as already massively informative through their bulk and occasional redundancy, the latter being of prime necessity in valid generalization.

Biological Investigations

The earliest returns were from the biological sciences; A. Woodbury, *et al.* (1958) compiled a preliminary check list of the species of the entire area. The final list included data drawn not only from published material, but from unpublished research notes, unreported herbarium collections and other relatively obscure sources. The volume therefore contains check lists which combine information from many earlier published reports covering smaller areas with information made available for the first time. Additionally a complete bibliography and a unique history of the biological study of the region are include. As a source book for further biological research, the volume should have long usefulness. In subsequent studies Woodbury and his associates (various) made a more detailed sampling of the Glen Canyon itself, making their findings available in a series of special papers. Some new species were described, the range of others was clarified or more precisely bounded, and considerable was learned about zonal territorial restrictions of some mammals and reptiles; not all these findings have been reported.

Using the series of checklists and special biological studies as a base, Woodbury (1965) later undertook an interpretation of the human ecology of the canyons. He drew upon published ethnobotanical studies and to a lesser extent upon Glen Canyon archaeological findings. His work, published posthumously, represents a halfway point in his study with many tantalizing gaps in analysis and interpretation. Even unfinished, the paper is provocative. It is true that Woodbury, knowledgeable as he was, cherished about the American Indian some highly subjective and stereotyped views not consonant with ideas held by anthropologists. He saw the Indian as a wretched, improvident creature engaged in a losing battle with a hostile world against which his technology was inadequate. Woodbury's conception of the whole of American Prehistory, including that of the Southwest, was somewhat outmoded as well. He correctly saw man in some contexts as parasitic upon a variety of obvious species, but even so, man's role in the ecosystem is for Woodbury evidently an entirely passive one. Man comes through in his writings as a "given condition," rather than as an active agent in the ecosystem. His views are reflected in the 18 pages given to section "Difficulties of Aboriginal Life," as opposed to the 11 pages allotted to "Adjustment to Environment." For Woodbury the "Difficulties" were those afflictions and diseases the individual might contract, ranging from hay-fever and other allergies through endo-, ecto-, and free living parasites to a dozen endemic diseases such as tularemia, tick fever, rabies and ornithosis. Anthropologists, as well as ecologists, rarely think of disease in connection with prehistoric populations, and Woodbury's emphasis thus adds a specific new dimension to ecological analysis. As a new avenue of study, for example, one can properly ask now: What medicinal plants available locally or by import can be shown to ameliorate (or specifically cure) the infections believed by Woodbury to be indigenous? If man is a crucial vector in the life cycle of the infecting organisms he should then perhaps be credited with important and presumably deleterious effects upon other mammalian species through the introduction of new diseases when he entered a previously closed system. In describing aboriginal adjustment to the canyon environment, Woodbury contents himself by listing the known and probable uses of many mammalian and floral species in a very general way. In his view, the gardens of the aborigines would have made little, if any change in the ecological conditions.

The heavy continuous seasonal collecting of wild species from "canyon bottom to mountain top" impressed Woodbury and received emphasis, but he made no attempt (other than to comment upon the negligible effect of gardening) to assess the place of man as an active agent in the Canyon Lands ecosystem. In sum, it seems fair to say that Woodbury's contribution lies with the emphasis upon parasites and endemic diseases as this brings out a rarely considered facet of prehistoric human ecology. At present, one cannot draw definitive or demonstrable inferences bout prehistoric debility or death caused by the probable endemics. Heightened awareness of the questions could, however, lead to specific study of the matter. Out of such study, sharper insights would conceivably emerge, although one cannot at present say just how or what these might be. A study of fecal matter in search of evidence of internal parasites in Glen Canyon collections is currently in progress.

Historical Investigations

Turning to recent history, we can see the total gains to knowledge as greater than in any other field. The reason for this is simply that no serious historical study of the region had ever been undertaken until the salvage program was initiated, but now it is possible to say that for the Glen, Cataract and San Juan canyons the historical data are richer than for any river in the west (Crampton, various). His several technical studies list about 270 historical sites on the Glen, Cataract, Narrow and San Juan canyons. More than half of these fall within the full-pool limits of Lake Powell and most have been lost beneath the lake waters. So many sites attest a far greater activity within the isolated canyons than would at first glance appear likely. The historic sites range through inscriptions left by early explorers, debris and other evidence of mining operations, trails from the canyon up to the slickrock plateaus, physiographic forms which are famous named landmarks and have historic overtones in some way or other, a few deserted buildings and other flotsam of man's passage. Taken singly, no one of these sites, unless it be the Hole-in-the-Rock Trail (D. Miller, 1959) or Stanton's ill-fated gold dredge (Crampton and Smith, 1961) is very impressive. Together, however, they etch an exciting picture of the withered dreams and disappointments, and rare successes, of an army of men who sought fame or wealth in a variety of ways in the Canyon Lands.

The recent history is easily divided into three phases, phases that are generally applicable to most rivers in the West although the sequence and timing would vary. Based on a preliminary study (Crampton, 1959) and later modified (Crampton, 1964d), these phases fall into an Exploration period, 1776 to about 1880; an Exploitive era, 1800 to 1920; and a Reclamation-Recreation phase, essentially beginning with Powell and unabated today, but falling primarily in the 1900–1922 span when adventurers, romantics and nature lovers coursed the area and cataloged its endless wonders—Natural Bridges, Rainbow Bridge, many archaeological sites and scenic wonderlands. The explorations by explorers began with the famous Escalante-Dominquez trek in 1776 from Santa Fe, New Mexico, in search of an avenue to the West Coast. Following them on even yet ill-charted paths, were fur traders, slave buyers and general traders who came to know Canyon Lands. Apparently only one, D. Julien, can be proved to have followed the Colorado River or its tributaries, but the whole of southern Utah and northern Arizona became better known through the restless travel of this group.

Exploration by government expeditions to north and south—the names here are Fremont, Simpson, Sitgreaves and Whipple—impinged upon the Canyon Lands as railroad surveyors, geographers, cartographers and artists during the two decades between 1840 and 1860. Mac-Comb and Newberry actually entered the Canyon Lands near the confluence of the Green and Colorado. Their work and discoveries still left the Canyon Lands blank on the map; inevitably it too must be explored. Here the incredible Powell—engineer, scientist, poet and prophetic visionary—matter-of-factly appears. With wooden boats and a handful of men he ran the Green and Colorado rivers, thus in 1869 placing the Colorado on the list of known rivers. In some sense, the era of exploration was over, but Powell returned later and was followed by the Wheeler and Hayden expeditions. These resulted in the acquisition of much detailed knowledge of the region by 1879.

Overlapping with the official explorations, there were the more prosaic discoveries of Mormon colonizers and missionaries who crossed the canyon. Hamblin became famous as an explorer and missionary to the Hopi and as peacemaker. Lee, who operated Lees Ferry, is another from this era. The activity of these and other men covered a period of about 25 years from 1854 to 1880. The series of Mormon thrusts climaxed with the Hole-in-the-Rock expedition (D. Miller, 1959) in the course of which a wagon train crossed the roughest part of the canyon country. Neither this foolhardy group nor the earlier ones were interested in the Canyon Lands. Their concern was finding passages through it. Although the river could be forded at many points, the problem was access roads on both sides of the river at feasible ford or ferry sites. Only four such sites developed—Lees Ferry, Hole-in-the-Rock, which son gave way to Halls Crossing, and Dandy (Hite) Ferry. The best access was to Lees and Dandy, and they soon came to draw most of the traffic. Before wagon traffic, of course, the ancient "Ute Trail," a ford near Kane Creek for horsemen—used by Escalante in 1776—was well known to travelers.

But no one yet viewed the Canyon Lands as useful, or potentially valuable except the occasional stockman who sought new grazing

68

Fig. 24. Remains of a water wheel used for mining purposes at Olympia Bar on the Colorado River, Glen Canyon.

Fig. 25. The Stanton Dredge in Glen Canyon.

Fig. 26. Remains of two oil wells, Kane County, Utah.

lands, and the expanding Navajo tribesmen who also were seeking
room for their flocks. Then, led by Cass Hite, a new wave of explorer-
exploiters arrived in 1883. These were the prospectors and promoters
who swarmed all over the west as one rumored gold or silver strike
after another lured them on. For the first time, Glen, the San Juan and
all the tributary canyons were followed out. The time, money and effort
of the gold-seekers were wasted. There was gold in the gravel terraces
along the Glen but the flour was too fine for commercial recovery techniques of the day (Fig. 24). The most famous of the losers was Stanton,
an engineer-promoter who assembled a huge dredge in the canyon after
hauling it piecemeal from the railroad at Green River, Utah, and down
into the canyon, a venture which earned his backers nothing (Fig. 25).
It was this same Stanton who surveyed the Glen to find a railway route
to the west coast. Others searched for oil during these years. Although
there were several waves of prospectors, the gold fever was spent by the
early 1900's. Sporadic flurries continued with a second search for oil
during the 1920's, and the uranium fever of the 1950's. And in the 50's
too, rich oil reserves were tapped on the edges of the Canyon Lands.
So it can be correctly said that the prospecting never really stopped
(Fig. 26).

The energy and ingenuity the prospectors displayed is astonishing. Everywhere one sees evidence of their presence; initials in an Indian ruin far up a canyon, abandoned equipment amid ragged pits on a gravel bar, a crumbling shack or deep cut steps slanting up the cliffs from a gravel terrace all testify to their detailed search as well as their blasted hopes. The distances from supply bases, the lack of local population, and the roughness of the country itself—all made the herculean but hitherto unsung efforts of these men the more remarkable.

The influx of the romantics began shortly after 1900. Through the wanderings of Douglas, Cummings, Bernheimer and others, the natural wonders of the whole Canyon Lands section were rediscovered, but this time they were publicized so that all Americans became aware of the tangled canyons, their scenic riches and the existence of such marvels as the Natural Bridges, Rainbow Bridge, the ruins of Betatakin and Kiet Siel, Arches and Monument Valley. Soon after being reported in popular and scientific periodicals, these national treasures were preserved as national monuments. The trend to recognize the scenic natural values was climaxed in the naming of Lake Powell (one wonders if Powell would have approved) and in designating its shores a National Recreational Area, an area enjoyed by just over one-quarter million people in 1965, with twice that number predicted for 1966.

Thus, the Glen and its environs are now known to have seen the recent passage of many adventurous and hardy men. Their history adds depth and another colorful chapter to recent western history. But the Glen has always been a lonesome place. Crampton (1964d) closes a summary volume by saying, "The sharpest focus . . . was still fixed on the area around the edges . . . " So, oddly, the Glen and San Juan canyons are paradoxically the focus of modern history less because of their own worth than because they impeded the march of conquest. Until the recent study, they were only known about, not known.

Archaeological Investigations

While the paragraphs above barely hint at the historical and biological findings available in the dozen technical reports, representing a wealth of new—at least coherently synthesized—data, the expenditure of effort in collecting archaeological data exceeded that in other fields. For this there are obvious reasons. There were more archaeological stations—usually called "sites"—to be found by plodding searchers, than any other class of data. Although the precise location of over 2000 sites is now known, there are undoubtedly scores of buried or well-hidden sites not discovered and now forever lost. This slow search itself took much time; and archaeological excavation requires even more time because it is arduous and slow and is done by hand. The archaeological excavation crews remained isolated deep in the canyons for weeks at a time. Their logistic support was time-consuming and difficult; also, the scholarly burden on the archaeologists was heavier because they followed decades of rumor. They were searching not only for new sites but were enjoined to verify the legends, grown up since Powell, of riches that never were. Therefore, as has been emphasized elsewhere (Jennings, 1963b; Jennings and Sharrock, 1965) the archaeologists were engaged in refining knowledge—actually clipping the wings of rumor and speculation, and correcting misconceptions—because in some ways the archaeology had had considerable attention, albeit in many cases, of poor quality. This scientific task of reevaluation, or achieving more reliable data and attempting a larger view, set problems very like those the biologists faced but on a different scale. For the historians, on the other hand, there was almost no history to correct or reassess. Theirs was a journey of first discovery—finding, understanding and reporting at last—a myriad of unremembered men and places, and assigning them a proper niche in the story of the west.

In any case, the contributions of the prehistorians are numerous. Particularly is this true if one includes the ancillary studies required by the archaeologists in extension or refinement of their own findings. Among the ancillary studies are palynology, dendrochronology, sedimentation, plant identifications of cultigens and utilized plants. Not new but invaluable, were the yeomen services of chemists, paleontologists, mammalogists, botanists and others.

Among the interesting new insights into Anasazi life resulting from the Glen Canyon work is some unexpected data on agricultural practice having to do with irrigation. That the Pueblo understood water collecting and storage and distribution is known from Mesa Verde (G. Stewart, 1940; Rohn, 1963; Herold, 1961) and Point of Pines (R. Woodbury, 1961); others are known at Mug House and Hovenweep and in the Zuni area. In Glen Canyon a masonry dam (Sharrock, et al., 1961a), a series of stone lined ditches (Lindsay, 1961a) and agricultural terraces (Adams, et al., 1961) were recognized and described. The masonry dam, if correctly identified, is a unique structure; it is a double-walled, U-shaped dam built across a short gully in the impermeable Chinle formation. There was evidently a spring channel in the Chinle and some subsurface water may have flowed along a large dune which rested upon the Chinle. At one end of the masonry enclosure, a water

Fig. 27. Double-walled masonry dam at Creeping Dune. Watergate at base of far wall.

gate or outlet with an adjustable flow setting released the stored water to a ditch system. Nothing resembling this has been elsewhere reported (Fig. 27).

The use of land-conserving terraces, linear borders and distribution ditches has been reported, but at Beaver Creek, an entire ditch and field complex was discovered and described. Successful gardening of the area involved diversion of water to the upper edges of an alluvial fan by ditch, the building of terraces and the maintenance of a series of stone lined ditches. Flow was apparently regulated by a series of notched slabs which are thought to have served to check both volume and velocity of flow. The excavators reckoned that the farm land supported a community of over 20 household units; this implies fewer than 100 persons, even if all the rooms were dwellings (Figs. 28, 29, and 30). And, at Castle Creek, not too far from Beaver Creek, there is a masonry aqueduct supporting an open ditch leading water from the creek to a large area of rich alluvium terrace above the creek bed. Lindsay, et al. (1965) mention several other irrigated areas, where canals can still be seen, on the south side of Navajo Mountain.

Further downstream in the lower Glen, other terraces, where sub-irrigation was feasible, were discovered (Adams, et al., 1961). These

Fig. 28. Stone-lined ditch at Beaver Creek.
(Museum of Northern Arizona photo.)

Fig. 29. Section of stone-lined
ditch with three notched slabs *in
situ*, Beaver Creek site. (Museum
of Northern Arizona photo.)

Fig. 30. Close-up of notched
slab *in situ*, Beaver Creek site.
Museum of Northern Arizona
photo.

Fig. 31. Prehistoric steps (on left) cut into slickrock.

terraces were in Aztec Creek, where masonry retaining walls had been built on bare Kayenta formation ledges along the stream. Behind the walls, the limited earth was retained, moist even today from seep from the Kayenta-Navajo contact line. Some or even all of the soil retained behind the walls was probably placed there when the terrace was created. Such land conserving terraces are common on the slopes of Navajo Mountain (Adams, *et al.*, 1961) and can be regarded as a standard feature of Kayenta agriculture as well as that of Mesa Verde. Further east, e.g., in the Bandelier area west of Santa Fe, these terraces are very common (Charlie Steen, personal communication), but only in recent years has their importance been recognized.

In terms of understanding the year-in/year-out use of the canyon, the great number and lengths of the aboriginal trails, including the hand and toe paths up the sheer cliffs, offer unexpected insights. These trails create a network of easy communication between canyon and highland all along the Glen. Adams, *et al.* (1961) casually report over 30 trails in the lower Glen Canyon (below the mouth of the San Juan). All of these are "clearly associated with historic or prehistoric" habitations. Some of this series occur in pairs, the older ones being conical or hemispherical holes, pecked into the cliff and now much weathered. Immediately alongside will be modern or historic trails up the naked rock, but consisting of flat steps hewn with steel tools, for the passage of animals—sheep, goats, mules and horses, as well as man (Figs. 31, 32 and 33).

Fig. 32. Closer view of pre-historic steps cut into slick-rock.

Fig. 33. Close-up of same prehistoric steps.

The new steps are credited to Navajo and Paiute (Adams, *et al.*, 1961; Crampton, various).

Ambler, *et al.* (1964) and Long (1965) devote considerable space to a consideration of the trails which lead northward from the highlands down into the canyon complex, and others which lead off the mesa top into the dissected lands to the south. In several cases the canyon trails go directly to, or pass close by, sources of lithic raw material where extensive chipping debris remains today. The author feels that these relationships can perhaps serve to equate the chipping site as coeval with the habitations to which the trails also lead or where they originate, thereby establishing a tenuous dating of the lithic sites where ceramic or architectural clues are lacking.

The Cummings Mesa (Ambler, *et al.*, 1964) trail system is important in its larger implication of frequent and easy communication in all directions from the agricultural community on the highest (southern) portion of the plateau. The trails argue that there was habitual travel from one center to another, to say nothing of wide ranging hunting and collecting trips, and we can postulate a vast network of now forgotten trails (some routes were metamorphosed into modern stock or pack trails or primitive roads) over the whole Kayenta land and the rest of the Pueblo domain (see also Reed, 1964b). The ease and frequency of intervillage contact observed ethnologically has apparently never been fully appreciated or sufficiently stressed as being equally true in prehistoric times, but the highlighting of the Glen Canyon region trail system puts emphasis on an important ecological and sociological point—the canyon dwellers were not confined to the canyons. In addition to well-defined trails, there is clear evidence that some canyons—Smith's Fork (Lipe, *et al.*, 1960) and Blocked Draw (Sharrock, *et al.*, 1963)—were well known and heavily used avenues in and out of the canyon complex. (See also Long, 1965)

This concern with trails and communications exemplifies an interest all the Glen Canyon reports reveal in what can be called ecology. (Of course, to some degree this is a current intensification of an older trend that is reflected in much recent archaeological writing.) Nonetheless, all the Glen Canyon investigators have made ecological notes and inferences which allow finer, more specific statements about the relationship of the inhabitants to the country and its resources. This aspect of the research can be seen as a positive, if general, contribution of the reported work. This interest manifests itself most frequently in the careful description of the setting (e.g., Lipe, *et al.*, 1960; Sharrock, *et al.*, 1963; Ambler, *et al.*, 1964), frequent allusions to climatic or environmental change (Schoenwetter, 1962; Schoenwetter, *et al.*, 1964) and other matters not yet subject to firm proof. More attention to ecologic nuances must, of course, begin in the field with the saving, during excavation, of much more "trash" of nonartifactual nature, to say nothing of closer observation of the terrain and biota. Lipe, *et al.* (1960) and Lance (1963) even speculate about the aggradation of the canyon and river sediment around the A.D. 1000's and its effects on the population as well as whether the human occupancy may have played some part in the accelerated aggradation. In Lance's (1963) interpretations of the deep sediments in Moqui and Lake canyons, he was particularly sensitive to alternate banding of the valley fill, and makes several suggestions as to a changing local precipitation regimen which would have immediate consequences for native gardeners, Sharrock, *et al.* (1961b, 1963) use archaeological evidence to make the same point, i.e., that vast loads of sediment were suddenly spread over the wide valleys of Lake and Moqui canyons, covering fields and certainly burying villages at Lyman Flats, Deadtree Flats and Red Ant Kiva. At the first two, bogs or marshes later formed over the site locations, presumably because of natural damming or beaver ponds. Modern beaver ponds were found in several of the better-watered streams (Figs. 34, 35, 36 and 37).

In another situation, at Benchmark Cave, Sharrock, *et al.* (1964) note an apparent rapid aggradation for 100 years or more on the main stem, including a flood of huge proportions (Fig. 38). The building up of the bar or terrace must have stopped at about the time the site was abandoned. Sharrock utilizes the rate of sediment accumulation in interpretation of the site. Long (1965) notes the occurrence of a pottery zone, dated at A.D. 1150–1225 (on the basis of included types) buried under sediment of considerable depth at site NA7376.

Slickrock Canyon was the object of a special study with an entirely ecological focus. The short canyon was unique in having not changed perceptibly since aboriginal times—so far as gullying or sediment loss or gain was concerned (Fig. 9). Also its floral inventory was astonishingly varied, being the longest list reported from any tributary. It also showed the heaviest aboriginal use (considering its short length and small area) of any tributary to Glen. There were two large ruins, Widow's Ledge and Mistake Alcove in cliff alcoves and numerous lesser sites of the same period (and an historic Navajo hogan) on the surface of the alluvium at present stream side, so it was certain that the canyon had not been flushed out or gullied since abandonment. To all appearances, this canyon could be taken as preserving, more or less intact, the same ecological situation it had presented to the prehistoric Pueblo.

78

Fig. 34. Immense falling sand dune in Moqui Canyon, ca. 600 ft. high and 800 ft. wide, covers Kayenta Formation and alluvial terrace.

Two aboriginal fields, it was thought, were still definable. One, below Widow's Ledge, was a pure stand of Old Man sagebrush (*Artemesia filifolia*), and another upstream was a pure stand of prickly pear cactus (*Opuntia*) (Figs. 14, 15). The latter is interpreted as a relict patch of this semidomesticate, but the sage is seen as subclimax vegetation having taken over a garden plot after its abandonment. Hundreds of soil samples were tested for variation in trace minerals or other evidence that the sage or prickly pear field soils differed from other areas of arable land. The tests proved inconclusive, so the entire matter remains speculative.

Already mentioned as being of paleo-ecological import are the reports from every canyon (except Slickrock) and the river itself, of the contrast between present and aboriginal times in the stream position and sediment depth. In the tributaries to both the Escalante (Gunnerson, 1959b) and the Glen the streams now run on ancient bedrock channels between either bare cliff or vertical banks of rich sediment up to approximately 100 feet deep (Figs. 35, 36 and 37). The stains of an-

Fig. 35. Buried sand dune exposed in alluvial terrace cutbank in Moqui Canyon.

cient soils or even flecks and bands of sediment mark all the canyon walls. Upon the now desiccated flats there gleam the whitened snags of ancient cottonwoods. In the sediment cliffs at least one deeply buried masonry wall was seen in section (Red Ant Kiva [Fig. 17]). In sheltered coves, where sediment remains, the sites occur at the level of the then floor of the valley. It is obvious that the now visible channels, long ago cut deep into the sandstone, were then deeply buried. The clear streams choked by beaver ponds and lined with trees and shrubs (see Lance, 1963), meandered across wide fertile flats where crops flourished on plots subirrigated by ground water, or even by simple stream diversion. Authors tend to agree that the "carrying power" of the canyon was then much greater and the population could have been far greater than the discovered sites would suggest. Jennings (1963b) suggests, as does Lindsay (personal communication), that many sites have been flushed out and that many more are buried and cannot be discovered. Also, Lindsay has noted site "loss" through sedimentation in the upland province. Lipe (various) minimizes the implications of the evidence and

Fig. 36. Alluvial terrace remnants exposed in falling sand dune.

Fig. 37. Horizontally bedded alluvial terrace; rock fall forms foundation at stream bed level.

Fig. 38. Twelve in. thick layer of white river-derived clay exposed in excavation trenches at Benchmark Cave. Trench sides were deliberately sloped
to avoid slumpage of soft sand. Strata above and below clay band contained artifacts.

believes that the sites known to us are essentially all there ever were and
that the population inferable from known sites is probably close to the
correct figure. Adams, *et al.* (1961) would perhaps agree with Lipe.
This is a debate which cannot be settled; it merely represents two
interpretations of the same information. The important thing is less a

question of who is nearest to the correct interpretation, than that this kind of observation and interpretation has been attempted.

In studying the sediments of Lake (Cooley, 1962) and Moqui (Lance, 1963) canyons, geologists have shown that there has been massive erosion and refilling of the major canyons several times in recent times, and speculate upon the many combined causes. My own view, largely derived from Schoenwetter (1962) and Lance (1963), is that one phase of aggradation climaxed about A.D. 900 and established an optimum setting for gardeners, a setting which later deteriorated by A.D. 1150–1200 when changing rainfall patterns—from winter to summer— set in motion another and more violent flood and up-building regimen that eventually caused the abandonment of the major canyons. The present bleakness is undoubtedly a function of the gullying of the past century. Lake Canyon, in fact, is historically documented as having been emptied in 1915 when Lake Pangarit breached its dam (Sharrock, et al., 1961b). In Moqui Canyon, at the buried Red Ant Kiva site (Sharrock, et al., 1963) there is conclusive evidence that gullying postdates the introduction of cattle; this perhaps supports Bryan's (1940) view that overgrazing hastened natural processes.

Of prime value in evaluating Glen Canyon findings is the work of the Museum of New Mexico in the Navajo Reservoir area of the Upper Colorado River Basin, in a series of discoveries of importance in understanding the history of the entire Southwest. The Navajo Reservoir is in the Four-Corners area, within what has been called the Mesa Verde branch or tradition sphere. From the emergency research there (Eddy and Dickey, 1961; Dittert, et al., 1963) a series of culture "Phases" has been recognized. In addition to an unnamed Archaic stratum, these are the Los Pinos, dated at A.D. 1–400, Sambrito, A.D. 400–700, Rosa, A.D. 700–900, Piedra, A.D. 850–950 and four later ones. All except the Los Pinos and Sambrito represent refinement in description or definition of already known occupations. The two earlier phases are extremely important in evidencing the presence of surface dwellings, brown pottery, and small villages, uniformly located near arable lands, to say nothing of establishing a very early date (pre-A.D. 400), for corn horticulture in the area. The authors identify numerous artifacts of both phases as having been carried over from the precedent Archaic substratum, thus showing both Los Pinos and Sambrito as transitional into the Pueblo pattern.

The effect of these discoveries is to prove, once and for all, the extreme extent of the Mogollon diffusion in the first stages of Pueblo evolution. The brown pottery, the large pit houses of the Sambrito with

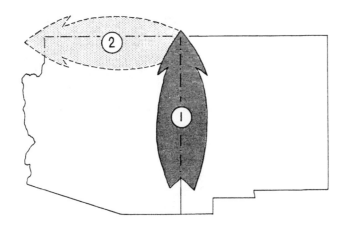

Fig. 39. Diagram showing early spread of Mogollon cultural traits northward (1) and later westward expansion (2).

entry ramps and some of the stone specimens show the Mogollon origin of the Sambrito beyond doubt. (See also McGregor, 1965). This new insight as to time of the southern influences on the northern Pueblo, coupled with the discoveries in the Kayenta area and the comparative studies of Aikens (1966b) and F. Lister (1964) throw altogether new light on the basic similarity of the Mesa Verde, Kayenta, Virgin and even the Sevier-Fremont subareas of the Anasazi. Some of the implications of these new data upon region-wide interpretation had been realized by McGregor (1965), but the extent to which the early spread of Mogollon traits simplifies and clarifies the story of the Southwest is not yet fully appreciated. Many discoveries of comparable impact may have been made in the past, but the simplifying effects of these make them particularly welcome. With McGregor, and possibly Reed, I would show the Mogollon axis as running N–S from the San Francisco Mountains to the Mesa Verde, soon (by A.D. 200 or 300) fanning out westward as far as Nevada (Fig. 39) with Mogollon traits, especially in architecture (houses *in* a pit, walk-in entry ramps, great variation in shape and size), being sometimes encountered in the Fremont and Sevier-Fremont as late as A.D. 1200 as far north as Nephi and Provo, Utah.

In connection with the Los Pinos structures some of the interpretations made by Eddy can be questioned. He identifies a scattered rubble of cobbles around some of the Los Pinos houses as "pavement" or an "apron." Based on the pattern at many open sites where masonry walls have tumbled or been pushed over, I think it is quite possible that the cobble patches are merely the evidence of very early experimentation with mudstone masonry, a trait apparent earlier in Mesa Verde than elsewhere in the Southwest. Day (1966) found similar "cobble aprons" which are unmistakably toppled walls originally made of large cobbles and adobe mortar. This is, however, a much later and distant occurrence, mentioned here only as another example of the sometime exclusive use of cobbles in Pueblo masonry construction. My argument also rests on the stratigraphy noted by Eddy. He states that the cobbles rest *upon* the refuse from the occupancy. Thus, the stones are the last deposit at the site and suggest no purposeful activity; the idea of collapse, even by slow "melting," of cobbles in crude mud mortared walls fits the stratigraphy, and the common sense mechanics of cobble masonry decay seems to better explain the facts. As other examples of the cobble aprons are found and carefully studied during excavation, this matter will become clearer.

In the same vein, Aikens's (1966b) comparisons of the Kayenta, Virgin and Four-Corners areas on the earliest time levels, are exceedingly useful. These reveal that significant regional variation did not begin until A.D. 900 or later. Aikens's views, summarized, are quoted extensively below:

> 3. Formal as well as functional similarities in cultural materials shared between the Kayenta and Virgin areas during the Basic Southwestern stage, and between them and more distant regions, suggest that the peoples of the Kayenta and Virgin areas did not at this period constitute discrete sociocultural groupings, but rather were participants in a uniform cultural pattern and sociological interaction sphere which had newly extended itself over the whole of the northern southwest, including the Mesa Verde, Chaco, Little Colorado, Kayenta and Virgin areas. In empirical terms, this is indicated by the fact that from approximately A.D. 500 to *ca.* A.D. 900, the pattern in valley environments of small, scattered settlements of circular, benched pit houses was almost universal in these areas. In ceramics, as in architecture, uniformity also prevailed, and a reduced-fired, black-on-gray ware with Lino style decoration was dominant over the entire northern Southwest. The Kayenta Lino focus, and the Virgin Muddy River phase, as ceramically and architecturally represented, are but local manifestations of this spread.
>
> 4. Based on an increased degree of formal differentiation in certain cultural features between the two areas during the subsequent Florescent stage, it is suggested that the Virgin and Kayenta peoples came to be separate sociocultural populations by approximately A.D. 900. They developed their own distinctive features in architecture and ceramics, and no doubt in nonmaterial areas of culture as well.

A high degree of interaction was maintained, but it apparently was not as intensive as formerly. Empirically, their cultural differentiation is demonstrated most strikingly by their almost mutually exclusive forms of unit pueblo architectural patterning—the circular or horse-shoe patterned room block dominant in the Virgin, and the straight-line or L-shaped block dominant in Kayenta. Too, ceramics were generally coarser in the Virgin than in the Kayenta, though essentially the same design styles prevail in both areas. Continuing cultural interchange is demonstrated by trade ceramics; interestingly, most of the influence seems to have been one way, from Kayenta to Virgin, though this may be due, at least in part, to the bias of archaeologists, who have for years considered the Virgin an offspring of the Kayenta and hence logically a receiver, rather than sender, of cultural impulses.

It may be noted here that the period *ca.* A.D. 900–1100 was a period of regional differentiation throughout the Anasazi area; the differentiation of Virgin and Kayenta from one another thus again fits as part of a general pattern, as did their essential nondifferentiation in the preceding period.

It may also be noted that this period in the Kayenta and Virgin areas, again as in the Anasazi areas as a whole, was a time of great population growth. The "Pueblo II expansion," as it has been called, has been thought of as a time of great movement of peoples into regions previously unoccupied. The evidence reviewed in this paper shows that, in the Virgin and Kayenta areas, at least, it was not so much a period of movement as a period of *in situ* population growth, with local populations in existence since Basic Southwestern times expanding out of the relatively few available valley environments into the surrounding, heretofore unoccupied, uplands. If this view of the "Pueblo II expansion" may be extended to the Anasazi Southwest as a whole, the Pueblo II period is cast in a new light. It is then not so much a period of migration into new areas, as has been thought, but a period of *in situ* growth of indigenous Basic Southwestern (or Basketmaker III) populations which had earlier spread thinly across the Anasazi Southwest, occupying at that time only the most favored valley environments.

5. By approximately A.D. 1150, the Virgin subculture ceased to exist. The fate of its bearers remains uncertain; it seems reasonable that they moved southeastward to join their relatives in the Kayenta region, but there is no clear-cut evidence of it. After A.D. 1150, the culture of the Kayenta region reached its greatest florescence,

culminating approximately A.D. 1300 in the great cliff pueblos of Kiet Siel and Betatakin, and numerous large, mesatop sites. Increments to this culture in the area of subsistence and subsistence technology included the kidney bean, the turkey, and the mealing bin; in the area of clothing, cotton and the loom were introduced; in the area of ceremony, the kiva first became truly widespread; in architecture, the advent of much larger structural aggregations was significant; and in the area of social structure, this aggregation of small structures into larger clusters, most clearly seen in the grouping together of a number of small, lineage-sized unit pueblos to form a large pueblo at the Segazlin Mesa site, marks the beginning of a transition from lineage to clan organization in this portion of the Southwest.

6. Throughout the Pueblo history of the Kayenta and Virgin regions, from early Basic (*ca.* A.D. 500) to late Florescent (*ca.* A.D. 1300), the most striking single feature is the *continuity* of the basic cultural pattern. This continuity is seen in the carrying through from the early Basic throughout the Florescent, of the same basic systems of social organization, subsistence and subsistence-related technology, ceremony and recreation, and clothing and ornamentation. Increments during the Florescent to each of these subsystems elaborated them somewhat, but worked no fundamental changes. The major cultural revolution to be noted in the entire span of Virgin-Kayenta development is the shift in social organization from autonomous lineages to interdependent lineages, or clans, which is seen in incipient form in the large late Florescent Kayenta villages.

The materials reported by Lindsay, *et al.* (1965) offer massive support for the conclusions reached by Aikens, and indeed, were heavily consulted by Aikens in the analysis.

In a study made about 1960, F. Lister (1964) insists that the Kayenta-Virgin dichotomy is spurious. Working entirely with ceramics she says, among other things: "Out of this restudy one firm thought has come: Kayenta pottery perhaps should be unshackled from the 'Virgin branch' and 'Johnson branch' notions: these are branches, it must be pointed out, that were defined ceramically and have no meaning in other aspects of the culture. It is now anticipated that work in southern Utah will allow us to suggest that both terms be discarded, that in their place the Kayenta branch ought to be regarded as including an unspecialized southern Utah sub-branch differing in pottery and in all other traits only in minor details. This view is strengthened by the finding along the right bank: the intensive regional specializations thought to exist in the Virgin River territory of southwestern Utah and the Johnson Lake Canyon country of south central Utah simply do not exist."

An abandonment of the spurious distinctions between the Virgin and Kayenta has obvious implications for the host of "cultures," that were originally distinguished from each other largely on ceramic grounds, in north, central and western Arizona. Their essential sameness, e.g., pit houses, above ground storage units and scattered small-settlement patterns, align them with the basic northern pattern far more closely than their variant ceramics set them off as "different."

Note here that all authors can agree on architectural settlement pattern and other distinctions between Kayenta and other centers *after* about A.D. 1100 (Aikens sees it as even earlier). Even the ceramic differences at this stage *seem* more real. The importance of seeing the Virgin-Kayenta as sharing a common lifeway in the early centuries of the Christian era lies in the recognition of an early Mogollon thrust which resulted in the dispersal of basic Pueblo culture over the entire northern Pueblo area, including, possibly, parts of central and east central Utah, before A.D. 500. If this be so, the reconstruction of migration routes and the statements about Pueblo II, instead of invoking territorial expansion carried on by actual migrant groups, can now be seen with the general similarities as a diffusion of this or that trait (including ceramic types) to extant and increasing populations. Why there should have been expansion after about A.D. 800 is not clear. While it can be credited to improved climate as more annual moisture or even more summer rain (Baerreis and Bryson, 1965) became available, the explanation may be found in improved or drought resistant strains of domesticated plants. Of course, the latter explanation is unproved, except as the dent corns may fill this requirement.

In opposition to the views above, on the other hand, there can be no doubt that late Kayenta expansion (mentioned earlier) through actual migrations can be defended for the twelfth and thirteenth and even fifteenth centuries. The best example of Kayenta thrust in the northern part of the Glen Canyon area is the Coombs site; Kayenta control of the entire Kaiparowits seems equally clear. The Listers (various) show that the Coombs site was a strong typical late Kayenta pit house village. Many smaller sites occur nearby as well. On the basis of pottery recovered, the site is reported as falling at about A.D. 1100, but it now appears that it could have been later. Similarly, the ceramics from the Kaiparowits (Fowler and Aikens, 1963) were assigned to the A.D. 1100 date. It must be remarked, however, that several of the pottery types found at both Coombs and on the Kaiparowits were thought, at the time the data were analyzed, to have a different lifespan than is now believed, and the actual dates of Kayenta occupancy may be as late as A.D. 1200 to 1250 or 1275. As mentioned earlier, Breternitz's (1963) work, as well as Ambler, *et al.* (1964), shows that the previously accepted lifespans for many named pottery types are much too short. In this case, the dating of the Coombs site is controlled by the presumed disappearance, by A.D. 1100, of Cameron Polychrome, Medicine Black-on-Red and Black Mesa Black-on-White. All the other types used in dating at the Coombs site either persist for centuries, cover a short span between A.D. 1050 and A.D. 1150, or occur after A.D. 1200. Ambler's analysis of the evidence on Cummings Mesa at site NA7498 involving the longevity of some of the same types used by the Listers at Coombs, would suggest a date nearer A.D. 1175 as the point at which the pottery type lifespans overlap. In any case, this site (or any other) *must* have been occupied until at least the beginning date of its included ceramics. Breternitz's findings permit a similar conclusion (but none of the above is hard and fast enough to constitute complete proof). We may, however, now be reasonably sure of somewhat later dates for the Kayenta occupancy of the Escalante-Boulder-Kaiparowits area than the A.D. 1100 suggested by the authors of the reports cited above. A.D. 1150–1175 or even 1200 now seems more congruent with the ceramic and other evidence as revised. What is more interesting about the "Kayenta push," if it exists, is that each of the heavily Kayenta areas outside the Navajo Mountain–Tsegi Canyon axis is a high, well-watered zone where no great evidence of earlier settlement has been discovered. This is even more interesting when we note Lipe's (1960) speculation that the Kayentans were the first immigrants (after Basketmaker II times) into the Glen Canyon itself (average elevation less than 4000 feet above sea level) in the A.D. 900–1100's with an apparent downstream withdrawal by A.D. 1200 and a Kayenta mingling with the Mesa Verdeans in the upstream and middle reaches of the canyon. Explanation for the Kayenta influx into the Kaiparowits and Boulder (Aquarius Plateau) highlands of the Glen are varied and unproved; better climate, population pressure, colonizing zeal all are variously invoked, but one cannot be sure.

One of the perennial questions in Utah prehistory (and one we cannot yet deal with) is how to explain the Fremont culture, its origins, content and relationships. The Glen Canyon researches have added data but little clarification. The range, shown in Fowler and Aikens (1963), according to F. Lister's (1964) ceramic identification should be extended south to the Colorado River, showing undoubted concentration at and around Escalante, Utah, and at Harris Wash (Fowler, 1963) in what is otherwise Kayenta country as shown in Fig. 23. At Coombs, 22 decorated (Ivie Creek Black-on-White) whole Fremont vessels were recovered, and 5 plain or corrugated gray specimens (a total of 10%) out of about 250 whole or restorable pieces from the site. A number of other Fremont types—some even from western Utah—are represented in the sherd collections. The Listers established, on the other hand, several Boulder area varieties of both Kayenta and Fremont types and established one or two new types as well. There seems to be little doubt, then, of trade, if not even more intimate late contact, between Fremont and the Coombs populations. The settlements around Escalante, south from Coombs, yielded more Fremont than Kayenta pottery types, as was true of the even more southerly Fremont enclave at Harris Wash. On the Kaiparowits, too, the mixture of Kayenta-Fremont ceramics is reported.

No generalizations about Fremont culture are warranted on the basis of Glen Canyon data, except as the extended limits of the pottery suggest more intimate contact between Kayenta and Fremont. The Fremont culture yet remains to be studied and understood; Fremont research, stimulated by Glen Canyon findings, is now being given emphasis in Juab Valley (Nephi, Utah), Uinta Basin (Roosevelt and Jensen, Utah) and along the Great Salt Lake (Plain City and Bear River, Utah).

Of widest interest to prehistorians is the extensive study of the "pure" Kayenta province by the Museum of Northern Arizona staff. On Cummings and Paiute mesas and on the Rainbow Plateau on the northeast flank of Navajo Mountain, these students have learned more about the Kayenta than all previous studies combined had produced. Many of their findings have been drawn upon in earlier paragraphs, but this section is specifically aimed at an added description of the Kayenta after about A.D. 900 (see also Aikens, 1965b, 1966b) because this is nowhere else available.

Aside from the ceramics, which are distinctive and appear to have been widely copied, and which have fairly reliable time span ascriptions (much less precise than formerly thought as a result of the Museum of Northern Arizona researches), the Kayenta has not been very well understood. How little was known began to be apparent when Bliss and Ambler (Hobler, 1965) demonstrated that a common, possibly the preferred, Kayenta dwelling was the pit house. Ambler was able to show extensive pit house use as late as A.D. 1270, at the close of the Pueblo III times, whereas Bliss, after some emergency work in the Klethla Valley asserted that probably 90% of Kayenta Pueblo dwellings were pit houses. While Beals, *et al.* (1945) mention pit houses, they were usually regarded as restricted to small Pueblo II sites. Thus, the repeated discovery of sites (e.g., Surprise Pueblo [Ambler, *et al.*, 1964]; also NA 5737 [Lindsay, *et al.*, 1965]; [Sharrock, *et al.*, 1964]) where the dwellings are pit houses, with above ground masonry structures, most probably granaries, lasting until the close of Pueblo III times, necessitates a new conception as to Kayenta architecture. The discovery of continued pit house popularity in the Kayenta district is not entirely unexpected, when one considers the pit houses near Flagstaff, in Zion Park, and all over the Fremont–Sevier-Fremont area of Utah. Most of these semisubterranean dwellings have been misinterpreted as kivas until the past decade (Meighan, *et al.*, 1956; D. Taylor, 1957). It would actually be more remarkable to find the pit house lacking in Kayenta, than to find it present and popular. The important thing is that its presence is now demonstrated, and the uniform continuous use of the pit house over an 800–900 year period in the western Anasazi region is firmly established. This fact calls into question many of the generalizations about the Kayenta, made on the basis of available survey or other superficial data, because a corollary of the pit house dwelling is the above ground masonry granary complex. The reality of wide-spread occurrence of a cluster of small, contiguous surface masonry units, near or encircling one or more pit houses is now recognized as a Kayenta trait, that is no less true beyond the Kayenta borders. Identical patterns occur in southwestern Utah, at every site excavated in the Sevier-Fremont and several sites in the Fremont area east of the Wasatch in Utah. Many of the small one- or two-room "unit dwellings" over the entire north half of the Southwest are most probably no more than granaries, adjunct to an as yet unnoticed pit dwelling. Thus the many references to "contiguous surface masonry rooms, fronting on a kiva" are in error (Day, 1966). Moreover, circular underground kivas enjoy only a limited distribution, and outside the Mesa Verde area are quite late.

But there are other Kayenta architectural data not previously well documented which can be cited. Apparently two standard settlement arrangements can be readily recognized. One is the plaza; the other the courtyard. They are described thus (Lindsay, *et al.*, 1965):

> Plazas in the Kayenta area occur in open sites, and not at cliff shelters. These shelters lie opposite, usually east of a central room block, comprising two or more masonry room structures. The plaza is further delineated on two sides by jacal and masonry walls extending from the

central block of rooms. The fourth side is normally walled, with a gap near the midsection to provide an entry to the plaza. Masonry and jacal rooms and pit houses are often built onto the sides of the plaza in external placement with doorways built into the walls to provide direct access to the plaza. Occasionally, rooms are placed directly in the plaza area. The ground plan of the plaza is rectangular or D-shaped. The floor is level or undulating, either bedrock or a difficult to define sandy surface which is variable in height, but nearly always below the room door sills. A kiva(s) is located in the plaza near the center or at one edge. In cliff sheltered structures, walkways or stairs occur and it is possible that these may have governed the function of a plaza as the subterranean kivas are usually located along these areas. The function of the plazas known to date is difficult to ascertain from excavated evidence. Plaza areas yield mostly indications of secular activities in the form of lithic debris from tool preparation, minor numbers of tools—usually found along walls; and occasionally hearths or cists, house sweepings in the form of trash lenses and broken pottery are not found in large numbers relative to rooms and courtyards. There have been no significant architectural recoveries from the plaza floors or subsurface deposits, nor is there any indication that more than a small section of a plaza was roofed. From the direct proximity of the kiva we might infer a predominantly religious function for the plaza, but this is an assumption based mostly on analogy with ethnographic situations. It is worthy to note that plaza oriented sites have few or no courtyards, and conversely, sites that are courtyard oriented have thus far no formalized rectangular plazas.

NA5815 and NA7498 provide excellent examples of plaza sites.

Courtyards in the Kayenta area are very common during the Pueblo II and III periods and have been recognized by this name at numerous sites, in both open and cliff locations. A courtyard is an open area lying in front or to the side of one or more domestic rooms. The floor space of a courtyard area is enclosed by one or more low masonry walls and in certain cases, a jacal wall. The side of the courtyard opposite the doorway(s) or the room(s) is frequently left open or when walled it is provided with a wide entryway. One or several doorways may enter the courtyard from rooms around its perimeter. The ground plan ranges from oval and circular to rectangular shapes. Courtyard floors are normally compacted walking surfaces on sand, occasionally clay and slabs or roughly smoothed and leveled bedrock exposures. Floors are sometimes laid on specially prepared platforms where leveling is necessary at both cliff and open sites, but the common form of preparation appears to be little more than hasty preparation of a space adjoining a structure. Total square footage of floor space for the majority of courtyards is far less than that of a plaza, although few courtyards are larger than the smallest plaza investigated thus far. The ground surface of the courtyard may lie below, even with, or above the adjoining room floors. Kivas are rarely associated with courtyards and in the few instances known, the association and arrangement of structures is not similar to that for plazas. Rooms may cluster about the courtyard and two or more courtyards may appear as a series, each associated with one or more rooms. Each grouping of associated rooms and a courtyard we have called a *Courtyard complex*. A number of courtyard complexes of varying sizes may form a pueblo or a community when the complexes are distributed over a site or small geographic area. Several pueblos, each consisting of several courtyard complexes, may also form a community such as appears on Segazlin Mesa. Each courtyard complex probably served a segment of the population whether at a village, pueblo, or community. The function of the courtyard appears to be secular. Domestic activities are revealed by the kind and quantity of remains found in the area: the large amounts of domestic trash and debris from tool and food preparation and the common occurrence of hearths and milling implements on the floors. Upon the abandonment of adjoining rooms, some courtyards were used for trash dumps. The distribution of the courtyard and room complex is over a wide area from the lowland field houses to the upland multi-room pueblos and one-room field houses. . . . *It is almost universal in the* arrangement of structures at sites in the Tsegi Canyon. (Jeffrey Dean, personal communication.) The distribution of sites with plazas is limited to highland sites simply because large multi-room pueblos were not built in the lowlands. Courtyard complexes of various forms are best illustrated in this report at the sites on Segazlin Mesa.

While these definitions and distinctions are valuable they do not bring out the additional fact that most sites are small, involving one to four structures, and that they are either linear (even the pit house villages may be linear in arrangement [e.g., NA5737, Lindsay, *et al.*, 1965]) or L-shaped, and that even large sites—i.e., Segazlin Mesa—are less integrated communities than *aggregations* of little site units. Aikens (1966b) has touched on this point. The fact that one can see the pueblo or homestead unit settlement pattern preserved, even in large concentrations, argues, it seems to me, against the oft inferred changes in social organization from Pueblo II to Pueblo III times. It seems that the social or kinship base must have remained the same throughout Kayenta cultural span, with some other as yet unrevealed explanation to be invoked as explanation for the late large centers, especially Betatakin and Kiet Siel. Whether there is any real justification for postulating social organization from *any* settlement pattern can be debated, of course, but these new data on standard homestead patterns permit speculation to be based on fuller and far more representative data than in the past. If the small settlement is taken as proving a family or extended family as the effective social unit, we can now argue that this persisted throughout the centuries of Kayenta life. In modern times the Hopi villages are groups of family houses built of usually contiguous rooms. One could identify the villages not as communities but as aggregations of family homesteads. The upland villages of the Kayenta lead Lindsay (personal communication) to a different view:

> . . . The Segazlin Mesa settlement includes a complex of contemporaneous pueblos, indeed an aggregation of household (domiciliary-storage-ceremonial) units, ranging from 1–2 rooms to 13+ rooms per unit, situated on a small mesa whose easiest route of access if "guarded" by a pueblo (NA4075) of 12+ rooms and 2 incorporated kivas. The aggregate to my view is evidence for the interpretation of a functional cohesiveness which I would term a community, including also other relateable sites as well into this complex. I realize this may be a questionable practice. Further, during Pueblo III, especially late, I would suggest that the forest of small sites may be obscuring the trees. In my mind there is not much difference in the size of the contemporaneous large sites, Red House, Yellow House, Pottery Pueblo, Segazlin Mesa, Inscription House, Betatakin, Kiet Siel, etc., but the village layouts do differ, however. In sum, I don't think that the large sites can be given a secondary position because of the large numbers of small sites. Nucleation is a trend in the Anasazi and it can be traced from Pueblo I times to the termination with abandonments in Pueblo III. I believe that a case could be made in the Kayenta area for the secondary status of the small sites (1–4 roomers) in middle and late Pueblo III. I agree with your reluctance at present to cast any sociological inferences.

A unique architectural trait, seen in both lowland and highland sites, apparently highly characteristic of Kayenta, is the entrybox. This is a practical device that is just what it sounds like—a slab enclosed pen

Fig. 40. Entrybox at
Bernheimer Alcove.

inside the house, extending from the doorway out into the room toward the firepit. It seems to have three functions—as a step down into the rooms, as a trash-dust collector, and as a deflector for the fireplace (Fig. 40), e.g., Bernheimer Alcove [Sharrock, *et al.*, 1963]). At certain lowland sites there are several examples of a series of flat slab stairways leading onto site ledges, into doorways, or into use areas (Fig. 41), (e.g., Widow's Ledge, Mistake Alcove [Sharrock, *et al.*, 1964].) Although the stone stairway is common at Kayenta sites, it also occurs at Mesa Verde Branch sites in quite elaborate stairway constructions. Many occur in Canyonlands National Park (Sharrock, 1966a).

Reported from upland sites only are instances of separate rooms— either pit house or surface structures—containing a battery (5 in Steer Palace, on Castle Wash [Sharrock, *et al.*, 1964]) of mealing bins, with no other interior features. They are sufficiently numerous that Lindsay, *et al.* (1965) set up a separate room category called *grinding rooms* (Fig. 42).

So far as construction techniques are concerned, no useful generalizations are possible. At any one compound or structure unit, there will be stone masonry and *jacal* walls—sometimes in the same building (e.g., Copter Ledge [Sharrock, *et al.*, 1963, Fig. 52]). Pit houses may be unlined, or may be plastered with adobe or there may be a slab lining or "wainscoting" at the base of the wall. Floors, too, vary through every

Fig. 41. Slab stairway at Widow's Ledge.

possibility. They may be unmodified sand, the bedrock, packed clay, flagstones, or even combinations such as an area of clay used to level off an otherwise bedrock floor. Room size and shape are variable, although granaries are more often smaller than dwellings. It seems that, while alignment of rooms and establishment of work areas and such matters were controlled by traditional or practical factors, the individual builder had a variety of equally acceptable techniques available to him. The choice may have rested on whim, or on available materials or some other practical consideration, such as the difficulty of digging a pit house in bedrock, although pit houses *are* common where sand or earth fill comprise the site location. The tradition of mixed architectural components is met, where stone for masonry is available, in both the lowlands and highland provinces.

Considerable detailed pit house architectural information came from the Bonanza Dune pit house data (Aikens, 1965b). Here, 22 pit houses, dated by ceramic finds at about A.D. 1100–1150, yielded almost every recorded variation on the pit house theme. There were floor

Fig. 42. Mealing bins grouped around a central firepit at Steer Palace.

partitions, slab lining, plastered walls, sealed subfloor sand lenses (as yet unexplained), evidence of "leaner" walls, and large chunks of these jacal walls, to name a few. The site, almost pure Virgin Branch cerami-cally, contained one near-classic kiva built late in the short life span of the site (Figs. 43, 44, 45 and 46).

Along with scores of other students, I have envisioned the "real" Anasazi as the vast settlements—in the Mesa Verde and vicinity, in Chaco Canyon, those on the Salt River drainage, the Little Colorado, and the upper Rio Grande—and have somehow shared with the early explorers of the Southwest an all-embracing contempt for that vaster area encompassing portions of four states where the grandeur was miss-ing. No one except Ferdon (1955) has yet ever seriously proposed that the large settlements were culture/religious/political centers that were supported by all the hinterlands. But, somehow the great towns occupy attention while the homesteaders receive scant study. The neglect of the insignificant or lesser sites has, I rather think, led to erroneous or dis-torted notions as to just what Anasazi or even the whole Southwest pat-tern really is. So possibly one major effect of the salvage of the Glen

Fig. 43. View of Bonanza Dune during excavation. Note extent and depth of site.

Canyon remains, and a concern with the contiguous Anasazi variants where relationships may be discerned, is to restore perspective.

All students know, but fail to remember, that over most of time and over most of its range the Anasazi and Western Pueblo were in no sense flashy, (e.g., Wendorf, 1956, or Haury, 1956). Other accounts uniformly comment upon drabness, smallness and artifactual poverty. For most of the Western Pueblo and even the Anasazi the basic settlement pattern was the small unit; the basic problem was livelihood. As Hunt (1955) implied for one small area, habitation zones no doubt shifted frequently (see also Lipe, 1960; Lipe, *et al.*, 1960; Sharrock, *et al.*, 1961b, etc.).

Architecturally there is great variation (Brew, 1946; Schroeder, 1955) and there exists no uniform or systematic step-by-step progression from brush shelter to pit house to clan unit house. There is no evidence of extensive contact, nor evidence that the big settlements set any styles except perhaps in pottery. Even the consuming religiosity of the Anasazi—as reckoned from kiva frequency and ethnologic analogs—can be denied, or at least debated for the hinterlands.

Fig. 44. Superposed structures at Bonanza Dune.

General Interpretations

The genius of the Anasazi culture, I submit, lay not in ceramics or other handicrafts nor architecture nor religion but in the ancient foraging skills to which was added horticulture. The evidence of Glen Canyon seems to me to argue that every member of the Anasazi population was quick to see and exploit almost momentary changes in moisture or other climatic change. In Glen Canyon, evidence points to exploitation on a more sophisticated scale than is usually acknowledged.

Most architectural forms in Glen Canyon and the tributaries are for food storage; few dwellings were found. For this lack of human housing there are two clear reasons. First in time there is the fact, beautifully documented (Fig. 17) in Lake and Moqui canyons, that many—perhaps most—of the dwellings are deeply buried and were not even visible to our surveyors (see Long, 1965; Sharrock, et al., 1963, 1964). The little villages must have occurred wherever there was enough fertile fill to permit crops. A contrary explanation has been offered that the canyon dwellers were a succession of farmers who did not dwell in permanent

Fig. 45. Another view of superposed structures at Bonanza Dune.

houses or who were even merely summer visitors. The point is not likely to be clarified now because of the second factor which is simply that most of the tributary canyons have been flushed out; the remains of the Pueblo houses of A.D. 900–1200 have gone down the Colorado, leaving only high alcove granaries or crude storage rooms and, rarely, a well-defined dwelling (Fig. 22). Thus, in Glen Canyon, we have recorded and studied storage structures and temporary shelters because that's what was left to see after 1) an aggradation (possibly general) and 2) a subsequent erosional cycle which emptied most of the side canyon silt, and its included archaeological data, into the turbulent river.

So it seems, perhaps, that continued reference to Glen Canyon as a "marginal" area where people came and went (which is of course true—one must assume continuous movement) is to miss the entire point. The fact that now seems to be important is that in Pueblo II time the Anasazi actually specialized in gardening in "marginal" areas, and that by understanding water and its conservation and use (and the idiosyncrasies of their crops), extended their domain into areas where neither then nor now is gardening truly feasible. This would leave the Glen

Fig. 46. Pole-impressed wall debris in structure at Bonanza Dune.

Canyon dweller not so much marginal as typical backwoods Anasazi—all of whom were working agricultural miracles in an environment which is today regarded as unfavorable for cultivation of crops without irrigation.

I suggest that efforts to correlate or connect the histories of the Kayenta, Virgin, Zion, Fremont, and Sevier-Fremont with the histories of the high centers not only wastes time but prevents the proper evaluation of the data we do have on their own terms. I have suggested elsewhere that the Utah Fremont and Sevier-Fremont (and I now include the Virgin and Kayenta) ought not to be judged as Anasazi but as a widespread archaic population selectively borrowing pottery, agriculture and varied architecture but never being full "inductees," so to speak, into Anasazi culture in anything beyond the material. This view may well not survive testing, but it is a fact that the descriptions one can compile from the literature of Kayenta, Virgin and Fremont all sound very much alike until A.D. 900 or 1000, as Aikens has shown. There is the nondescript and heterogeneous architecture over the full time span. There can be found the ubiquitous gray pottery, well nigh indistinguishable from area to area (Anderson, 1960, but *cf.*, Anderson, 1963) although it bears several local names. And Schroeder's (1955) work at Zion Park makes clear that the Zion villages are storage sites—not extensive villages, to say nothing of the more northerly Virgin affiliated sites at Garrison and Paragonah which likewise contained more food storage structures than dwellings.

No one seriously questions the existence of three culture centers in the American Southwest. Their relationships in time and their joint paternity in an Archaic substratum is not extensively debated. It is ironic, not to say tragic, that the first known Southwest culture—the Four-Corners Anasazi or Mesa Verde Anasazi and its dependent regional variants—is the least well studied, if one may judge by the literature available. Nonetheless, the cliff houses of the Mesa Verde, the huge open towns in the Chaco and the spectacular setting of de Chelly villages are seen even by scholars, to be the *real* Anasazi with the other related manifestations deemed inferior or of lesser significance.

But, if a culture is to be judged by its preponderant manifestations the Anasazi could best be understood by ignoring the great ruins. In a sense, the Southwest and the Maya field are alike. The Mayanists have studied epigraphy, architecture, astronomy, and art: the culture, as known to the Maya themselves, in great degree remains unstudied. Similarly, fortunes have been spent in the Southwest in emptying prehistoric apartments of sand and broken pottery, with the scientists unwilling to deal with the equally informative, infinitely more numerous ruins and other evidences of lesser physical bulk.

Because the large Pueblo towns yielded pots by hundreds and potsherds by tens of thousands, a heavy interpretive burden has been borne by ceramics. This emphasis remains with us even though the significance of the pottery for the users has never been a major point of concern. And what has fascinated me is that the big Southwest towns did not appear to represent any secular or religious dominance or a central political entity. They were just big towns in a sea of little ones and apparently represented nothing but concentrations of people. Haury (1956) has pointed out that water is the key to life, and explains the large towns as first, well watered; after this, all else is possible.

If, for a moment, one can forget the big towns but remember the water problem, the Southwest and especially the Anasazi empire has a different cast. The important fact about the Anasazi gardeners, it seems to me, is not their late tendency to congregate and build big villages where there was adequate water, nor in their architecture which was not at all sophisticated, but in their universal ability to develop and exploit *limited* water. What ought to be remembered (and what could dramatically shift the interpretation of Southwest prehistory) is that for most of the time the Anasazi were widely dispersed even during Pueblo III, except in the few centers of wide renown. For every large Kayenta village site of the magnitude of Kiet Siel there are a thousand little settlements. On the Mesa Verde itself little sites covering 1500 years of time exist alongside the fabled (and really not so large) cliff houses.

If it is desirable to appraise the Southwest Anasazi culture as a man-land-culture problem, as a problem in human ecology, or even as an exercise in reconstructing a culture where social organization was simple, the overall political and religious controls weak and tenuous, the people bound with loose or nonexistent social ties outside the lineage, then the high centers lose their importance and the focus shifts to the scattered farmsteads whose numbers are legion.

What is known already as to variation of the Anasazi? Students recognize the Mesa Verde-Mancos-Durango constellation. This and the closely related Chaco center make up a 1) Mesa Verde Anasazi. Westward, related but different, is the 2) Kayenta district. Influenced by Kayenta is the 3) Virgin branch and a 4) Fremont and Sevier-Fremont area has been suggested but not well documented as significantly dependent upon Anasazi influence except in ceramics and possibly the pit house. The agriculture may well be a result of Plains influence. Certainly the Fremont dent corn is not an Anasazi strain. (It was hoped that the vast collections of corn and corncobs from the Glen Canyon might shed light on the matter of Fremont dent origins, one of the minor, but vexing, problems in the history of maize. Although Cutler [1966] considers the problem, he can make no definitive statement. Apparently its route of introduction into the Arizona strip and thence to the Fremont province cannot yet be charted. We are left with the assumption that it may be a successful direct importation from Mexico, an import which was successful because of the highly adaptive qualities of this viable strain. In view of Aikens's [1966a] analysis of the Fremont, the Fremont dent corn may be derived from a Plains dent variety.) These districts/branches do not show influences proportional to distance; e.g., Fremont sites quite close to Mesa Verde resemble, ceramically at least, collections from the Kayenta or Virgin and Sevier-Fremont—not Mesa Verde. This has led Gunnerson (1960) to suggest that the Fremont is culturally descended from, or related to the Virgin Branch, although this view is not yet supported by other scholars.

In the minds of most other students there rests, however, the tacit assumption that the Mesa Verde is the hub, nub and center of inspiration for Kayenta and Virgin (and Fremont) ceramic styles, architecture and other traits. Tree-ring dates are not available from all the areas, and in this lack, and with all eyes turned toward Mesa Verde, the standard interpretation is that a pottery shape or design found in Kayenta or Virgin context resembling one from Mesa Verde, was derived from and hence was younger than the Mesa Verde counterpart. And of course the Basketmaker-Pueblo sequences, trait lists, and dates of phase duration all were established from Four-Corners Mesa Verde and Kayenta data at a time when that region was believed to be the font of inspiration for the entire Southwest. What I'm saying is that the traditional way of looking at and thinking about Mesa Verde-Kayenta-Virgin relationships has all the answers built in, and no new interpretations may be expected until the data enforce a new viewpoint.

As stated earlier, the Glen Canyon area cannot certainly be shown to have been much utilized by man prior to the Christian era. Restricted areas—notably Moqui Canyon, a few sites on the main stem and on the plateaus—show a Basketmaker II stage occupancy (Figs. 47 and 48). This latter use, aside from being scanty, was short, so that the canyon lands were apparently again relatively empty of permanent inhabitants until the era of so-called Pueblo expansion—Pueblo II and early Pueblo III stages. The Pueblo II and III stages are usually assigned to the years A.D. 900 to A.D. 1300. After these years the Glen Canyon and the vast lands around it seem to have been empty of human life for a time. However, incursions by Hopi, Ute or Southern Paiute and finally Navajo all up into historic times are evidenced. None of these later visitors can be shown archaeologically to have been either frequent or permanent.

Pueblo II and III as used here are not the Pueblo II and III of fable and legend, as synthesized by Southwest scholars since about 1925. These stages were first generally described in rather precise statements as possessing a cluster of standard traits which comprise the unique characteristics by which the stages can be recognized when these traits are found. The fallacy of this rigid use of typology and trait list has been cogently condemned for decades (Roberts, 1935, and Brew, 1946, among others). The Pueblo II and III stages which concern us here are indeed a far sorrier thing than the rich high culture envisioned by the early writers. Although Pueblo II stage "times" are widely identified with great Anasazi expansion—a spread over most of Utah, parts of Nevada and far to the east—there is less general comment that the Pueblo II complex which spread so widely is not a "classic"

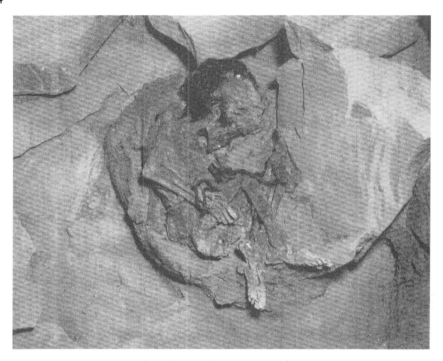

Fig. 47. Basketmaker infant burial, Bernheimer Alcove.

manifestation by any means. Gillin (1941) and Steward have both noted this but interpreted it far too chronologically. Pueblo II is a mixed model, a sort of unselected grouping of traits which constitutes a kind of blurred Anasazi. Steward (various) long ago noted the "mixed" traits which were blended to make "Utah Anasazi." By "mixture" Steward meant of course the anachronistic association of "early" and "late" traits. The ascription of "earliness" or "lateness," however, was a function of the trait descriptions of the several classic Basketmaker-Pueblo stages. Steward also interpreted chronologically some of the holdovers or anachronisms he observed, e.g., in the Paria Country, concluding on the basis of presence of pit houses and gray pottery that there were both Basketmaker II and Pueblo II stages with concomitant timespan represented by the ruins in the Paria area. It now seems that there is really but one agricultural occupation recorded in most of this area as well as the rest of the western region and that even Steward's latest explanations (1941) are not entirely accurate.

The approach here has been different from Steward's. In essence, Steward correctly recognized the Utah manifestations as being a blend

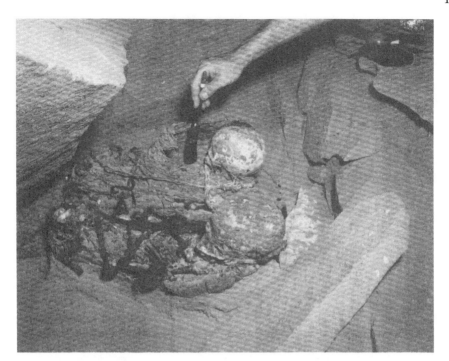

Fig. 48. Cluster of three Basketmaker infant burials, Bernheimer Alcove. The third burial is at the feet of and beneath the other burials.

or *melange* of traits elsewhere accorded much value as time indicators. His analytic approach was to identify various traits/complexes as to presumed timespan and explain Utah prehistory partially as a series of increments of traits which periodically diffused northwestward from the Anasazi centers. The picture was one of long occupancy of Utah with incomplete trait complexes diffusing differentially to form varyingly anachronistic combinations here and there about the "Northern Periphery" (Steward, 1933a, 1933b, 1936, 1941).

Present evidence makes a different interpretation possible, and more readily defensible. This position is merely that most of Arizona, all of Utah and eastern Nevada were in fact settled early—say by A.D. 300–400—from the south from the Mogollon or Western Pueblo center (see also Schroeder, 1965). Thus I would derive all the early backwoods Anasazi directly from the Mogollon before the florescence of the Four-Corners and other high centers came to pass. And I would ascribe the traits which appear in the larger western province neither to Kayenta nor Mesa Verde, but to an early southern heritage common to all. Thus, I am suggesting that there was no extreme Pueblo territorial expansion

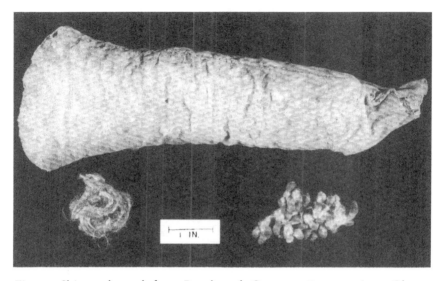

Fig. 49. Skin seed pouch from Benchmark Cave, 1958 excavations, Glen Canyon. On the left is the fiber plug and on the right are some of the cotton seeds found in the pouch.

Fig. 50. Whole ears of corn from Sheep Horn Alcove, Pantry Alcove and Triangle Cave, 1961 excavations, Harris Wash.

Fig. 51. Whole storage gourd, Curcubita mixta, from Triangle Cave, 1961 excavation, Harris Wash.

at a Pueblo II stage or "Pueblo II times," although there was undoubtedly a population increase. Conversely I am suggesting that the Pueblo II stage flavor did in fact diffuse more slowly over a vast area—once its special attributes existed—but that these diffused to an already widespread and simple static culture. This is not to say that local distinctions cannot be shown in the distance, say from Flagstaff, Arizona, to Willard, Utah, but in efforts to show significant cultural difference or to show direction of "influence," the full significance of the monotonous sameness of the basic patterns of architecture—i.e., longevity of the pit house, pottery styles, site location or settlement pattern, lack of readily identifiable kivas, pit house with associated surface storage rooms (masonry or adobe)—over the wide area seem to have been discounted unduly. My own tendency is to see the data evidence for a very early dispersal of a "basic" Pueblo pattern from southeastern Arizona and westernmost New Mexico over the entire area of Pueblo dominance to be little modified until the technological elaboration of the Mesa Verde–de Chelly–Chaco centers began to pulse outward irregularly and with differential acceptance. In this view the Fremont of Utah material becomes harder to explain. The two or three dated sites (Old Woman

[D. Taylor, 1957], by radiocarbon [Crane and Griffin, 1959], and Nine Mile Canyon [Gillin, 1955] by dendrochronology [Schulman, 1948]) seem to be later than A.D. 1000, so that no evidence of an early agricultural population can be adduced at present. Probably the Fremont culture will only be understood when students look at the evidence *without* the prior assumption that the Fremont is merely a dilute Anasazi. Aikens's (1966a) summary alignment of the Fremont with the Plains will provide a radically new basis for evaluating the Fremont evidence.

Conclusions

As a conclusion to this summary I can only reiterate what has been mentioned earlier: We entered the Glen Canyon expecting to find an easily documented, stratified sequence eof Southwest cultures from pre-Christian to historic times. We expected too much. That the archaeological findings fell far short of our imaginings is more a comment upon our experience, knowledge and judgment than a disparagement of the data as discerned. We left the canyon with a solid corpus of new data from a vast area, previously unknown (or unreported) to science—data that effectively removed the region from the limbo of the unknown. Instead of an empty place on the maps of biologists, historians and archaeologists as it once was, Glen Canyon emerges as the best known archaeological area of comparable size and difficulty in the West. This, as I see it, is the main contribution of the Upper Colorado River Basin Archeological Salvage Program, Glen Canyon Project.

Bibliography

Included in this bibliography are all known contributions to the Upper Colorado River Basin Archeological Salvage Program deemed significant enough for inclusion. Museum of Northern Arizona contributions are marked with one asterisk; University of Utah contributions are marked with two asterisks.

**   1963c Preliminary Report on Excavations in Southwestern Utah, 1962. *Utah Archeology: A Newsletter*, Vol. 9, No. 1, pp. 6–10. Salt Lake City.

**   1965a Appendix I: Surveyed Sites in the Virgin Valley and Johnson Canyon. *In* Excavations in Southwest Utah," C. Melvin Aikens. *University of Utah Anthropological Papers*, No. 76, *Glen Canyon Series*, No. 27, pp. 132–53. Salt Lake City, Utah.

**   1965b Excavations in Southwest Utah. *University of Utah Anthropological Papers*, No. 76, *Glen Canyon Series*, No. 27. Salt Lake City.

    1966a *Plains Relationships of the Fremont Culture: A Hypothesis Based on Excavations at Two Fremont-Promontory Sites in Northern Utah.* Ph.D. dissertation, University of Chicago, Department of Anthropology, Chicago.

**   1966b Virgin-Kayenta Cultural Relationships. *University of Utah Anthropological Papers*, No. 79, *Glen Canyon Series*, No. 29. Salt Lake City.

**Ambler, J. Richard
    1959   A Preliminary Note on 1959 Excavations at the Coombs Site, Boulder, Utah. *Utah Archaeology: A Newsletter*, Vol. 5, No. 3, pp. 4–11. Salt Lake City.

*Ambler, J. Richard, Alexander J. Lindsay, Jr., and Mary Anne Stein
    1964   Survey and Excavations on Cummings Mesa, Arizona and Utah, 1960–1961. *Museum of Northern Arizona Bulletin*, No. 39, *Glen Canyon Series*, No. 5. Flagstaff.

Anderson, Keith Maxwell
    1960   *Utah Virgin Branch Plain Utility Pottery.* MA thesis, University of Utah Anthropology Department, Salt Lake City.

*Adams, William Y.
    1959   Navajo and Anglo Reconstruction of Prehistoric Sites in Southwestern Utah. *American Antiquity*, Vol. 25, No. 2, pp. 269–72. Salt Lake City.

*   1960   Ninety Years of Glen Canyon Archeology, 1869–1959. *Museum of Northern Arizona Bulletin*, No. 33, *Glen Canyon Series*, No. 2. Flagstaff.

*Adams, William Y. and Nettie K. Adams
     1959   Inventory of Prehistoric Sites on the Lower San Juan River, Utah. *Museum of Northern Arizona Bulletin*, No. 31, *Glen Canyon Series*, No. 1. Flagstaff.

*Adams, William Y., Alexander J. Lindsay, Jr. and Christy G. Turner II
     1961   Survey and Excavations in Lower Glen Canyon, 1952–1958. *Museum of Northern Arizona Bulletin*, No. 36, *Glen Canyon Series*, No. 3. Flagstaff.

**Aikens, C. Melvin
     1961   *A Sketch of Kayenta Anasazi with a Comparative Trait List of Kayenta, Virgin Branch, Sevier-Fremont and Fremont Cultures.* Ms. On file University of Utah, Anthropology Department. Salt Lake City.

**   1962   The Archeology of the Kaiparowits Plateau, Southeastern Utah. MA thesis, University of Chicago, Department of Anthropology. Chicago.

**   1963a   Appendix II: Kaiparowits Survey, 1961. *In* "1961 Excavations, Kaiparowits Plateau, Utah," Don D. Fowler and C. Melvin Aikens. *University of Utah Anthropological Papers*, No. 66, *Glen Canyon Series*, No. 20, pp. 70–100. Salt Lake City.

**   1963b   Appendix II: Survey of Harris Wash. *In* "1961 Excavations, Harris Wash, Utah," Don D. Fowler. *University of Utah Anthropological Papers*, No. 64, *Glen Canyon Series*, No. 19, pp. 101–106. Salt Lake City.

Anderson, Keith Maxwell
     1963   Ceramic Clues to Pueblo-Puebloid Relationships. *American Antiquity*, Vol. 28, No. 3, pp. 303–307. Salt Lake City.

Baerreis, David A. and Reid A. Bryson
     1965   Climatic Episodes and the Dating of Mississippian Cultures. *The Wisconsin Archeologist, New Series*, Vol. 46, No. 4, pp. 203–20. Milwaukee.

**Bannister, Bryant
     1964   Beef Basin, Utah, Tree-Ring Materials. Addendum *In* "1962 Excavations, Glen Canyon Area," Floyd W. Sharrock, et al. *University of Utah Anthropological Papers*, No. 73, *Glen Canyon Series*, No. 25, pp. 173–75. Salt Lake City.

Beals, Ralph L., George W. Brainard and Watson Smith
     1945   Archaeological Studies in Northeast Arizona. *University of California Publications in American Archaeology and Ethnology*, Vol. 44, No. 1. Berkeley.

*Breternitz, David A.
1957 Heltagito Rockshelter (NA 6390). *Plateau*, Vol. 30, No. 1, pp. 1–16. Flagstaff.

1963 *The Archaeological Interpretation of Tree-Ring Specimens for Dating South-western Ceramic Styles.* Ph.D. thesis, University of Arizona, Department of Anthropology. Tucson.

Brew, John Otis
1946 Archaeology of Alkali Ridge, Southeastern Utah. *Papers of the Peabody Museum of American Archaeology, and Ethnology*, Vol. 21. Cambridge.

1961 Emergency Archaeology: Salvage in Advance of Technological Progress. *Proceedings of the American Philosophical Society*, Vol. 105, No. 1, pp. 1–10. Philadelphia.

Bryan, Kirk
1940 Erosion in the Valleys of the Southwest. *New Mexico Quarterly*, Vol. 10, No. 4, pp. 227–32. Albuquerque.

Bullard, William Rotch, Jr.
1962 The Cerro Colorado Site and Pithouse Architecture in the Southwestern United States Prior to A.D. 900. *Papers of the Peabody Museum of American Archaeology and Ethnology*, Vol. 44, No. 2. Cambridge.

Butler, B. Robert
1965 The Structure and Function of the Old Cordilleran Culture Concept. *American Anthropologist*, Vol. 67, No. 5, Pt. 1, pp. 1120–31. Menasha.

**Clark, Susan R.
1966 Tabular Summary of Plant and Animal Resources of the Glen Canyon. Addendum *in* "Corn, Cucurbits and Cotton from Glen Canyon," Hugh C. Cutler. *University of Utah Anthropological Papers* , No. 80, *Glen Canyon Series*, No. 30, p. 63. Salt Lake City.

*Colton, Harold S.
1962 Steamboating in the Glen Canyon of the Colorado River. *Plateau*, Vol. 35, No. 2, pp. 57–59. Flagstaff.

*Cooley, Maurice E.
1958a *Physiography of Glen and San Juan Canyons, Utah and Arizona.* (Multilithed, limited distribution.) Museum of Northern Arizona. Flagstaff.

* 1958b Physiography of the Glen–San Juan Canyon Area, Part I. *Plateau*, Vol. 31, No. 2, pp. 21–33. Flagstaff.

* 1959a Physiography of the Glen–San Juan Canyon Area, Part II: Physiography of San Juan Canyon. *Plateau*, Vol. 31, No. 3, pp. 49–56. Flagstaff.

*   1959b Physiography of the Glen–San Juan Canyon Area, Part III: Physiography of Glen and Cataract Canyons. *Plateau*, Vol. 31, No. 4, pp. 73–79. Flagstaff.

*   1960 Analysis of Gravel in Glen–San Juan Canyon Region, Utah and Arizona. *Arizona Geological Society Digest*, Vol. 3, pp. 19–24. Tucson.

*   1961 Description and Origin of Caliche in the Glen–San Juan Canyon Region, Utah and Arizona. *Arizona Geological Society Digest*, Vol. 4, pp. 35–41. Tucson.

*Cooley, Maurice E.
     1962 Late Pleistocene and Recent Erosion and Alluviation in Parts of the Colorado River System, Arizona and Utah. *U.S. Geological Survey Professional Paper*, No. 450-B, pp. B48–B50. Washington.

*   1964 Travertine Deposits in Glen Canyon Regions, Utah and Arizona. *In* "Contributions to the Geology of Northern Arizona," Harold S. Colton, et al. *Museum of Northern Arizona Bulletin*, No. 4, pp. 56–58. Flagstaff.

*   1965 Stratigraphic Sections and Records of Springs in the Glen Canyon Region of Utah and Arizona. *Museum of Northern Arizona Technical Series*, No. 6. Flagstaff.

*Cooley, Maurice E. and W. F. Hardt
     1961 The Relation of Geology to Hydrology in the Segi Mesas Area, Utah and Arizona. *Arizona Geological Society Digest*, Vol. 4, pp. 59–68. Tucson.

**Crampton, C. Gregory
**   1959 Outline History of the Glen Canyon Region, 1776–1922. *University of Utah Anthropological Papers*, No. 42, *Glen Canyon Series*, No. 9. Salt Lake City.

**   1960 Historical Sites in Glen Canyon, Mouth of San Juan River to Lees Ferry. *University of Utah Anthropological Papers*, No. 46, *Glen Canyon Series*, No. 12. Salt Lake City.

**   1962 Historical Sites in Glen Canyon, Mouth of Hansen Creek to Mouth of San Juan River. *University of Utah Anthropological Papers*, No. 61, *Glen Canyon Series*, No. 17. Salt Lake City.

**   1964a Addendum of New Data Relating to Areas Covered in Previous Reports. *In* "Historical Sites in Cataract and Narrow Canyons, and in Glen Canyon to California Bar," C. Gregory Crampton. *University of Utah Anthropological Papers*, No. 72, *Glen Canyon Series*, No. 24, pp. 65–72. Salt Lake City.

     1964b Historical Sites in Cataract and Narrow Canyons, and in Glen Canyon to California Bar. *University of Utah Anthropological Papers*, No. 72, *Glen Canyon Series*, No. 24. Salt Lake City.

** 1964c The San Juan Canyon Historical Sites. *University of Utah Anthropological Papers*, No. 70, *Glen Canyon Series*, No. 22. Salt Lake City.

1964d *Standing Up Country; the Canyon Lands of Utah and Arizona*. Alfred A. Knopf, New York; University of Utah Press, Salt Lake City in association with the Amon Carter Museum of Western Art. Fort Worth.

**Crampton, C. Gregory and Dwight L. Smith (eds.)
1961 The Hoskaninni Papers, Mining in Glen Canyon, 1897–1902, by Robert B. Stanton. *University of Utah Anthropological Papers*, No. 54, *Glen Canyon Series*, No. 15. Salt Lake City.

Crane, H. R. and James B. Griffin
1959 University of Michigan Radiocarbon Dates IV. *American Journal of Science Radiocarbon Supplement*, Vol. 1, pp. 173–98. New Haven.

*Creer, Leland H.
1958a The Activities of Jacob Hamblin in the Region of the Colorado. *University of Utah Anthropological Papers*, No. 33, *Glen Canyon Series*, No. 4. Salt Lake City.

** 1958b Mormon Towns in the Region of the Colorado. *University of Utah Anthropological Papers*, No. 32, *Glen Canyon Series*, No. 3. Salt Lake City.

Cressman, L. S.
1960 Cultural Sequences at the Dalles, Oregon. *Transactions of the American Philosophical Society, New Series*, Vol. 50, Pt. 10. Philadelphia.

**Cutler, Hugh C.
1966 Corn, Cucurbits and Cotton from Glen Canyon. *University of Utah Anthropological Papers*, No. 80, *Glen Canyon Series*, No. 30. Salt Lake City.

*Cutler, Hugh C. and John W. Bower
1961 Appendix: Plant Materials from Several Glen Canyon Sites. *In* "Survey and Excavations in Lower Glen Canyon, 1952–1958," William Y. Adams, Alexander J. Lindsay, Jr., and Christy G. Turner II. *Museum of Northern Arizona Bulletin*, No. 36, *Glen Canyon Series*, No. 3, pp. 58–61. Flagstaff.

Daifuku, Hiroshi
1952 A New Conceptual Scheme for Prehistoric Cultures in the Southwestern United States. *American Anthropologist*, Vol. 54, No. 2, pp. 191–200. Menasha.

1961 Jeddito 264; a Report on the Excavation of a Basket Maker III–Pueblo I Site in Northeastern Arizona with a Review of Some Current Theories in Southwestern Archaeology. *Papers of the Peabody Museum of American Archaeology and Ethnology*, Vol. 33, No. 1, *Awatovi Expedition Reports*, No. 7. Cambridge.

*Danson, Edward B.
  1958   The Glen Canyon Project. *Plateau*, Vol. 30, No. 3, pp. 75–78. Flagstaff.

**Day, Kent C.
  1961   Archeological Survey and Testing in Moqui Canyon and Castle Wash, 1961. *Utah Archaeology: A Newsletter*, Vol. 7, No. 4, pp. 12–14. Salt Lake City.

**   1963a Appendix II: Moqui Canyon and Castle Wash Survey. *In* "1961 Excavations, Glen Canyon Area," Floyd W. Sharrock, Kent C. Day and David S. Dibble. *University of Utah Anthropological Papers*, No. 63, *Glen Canyon Series*, No. 18, pp. 237–305. Salt Lake City.

**   1963b Preliminary Report of the Flaming Gorge Survey. *Utah Archeology: A Newsletter*, Vol. 8, No. 4, pp. 3–7. Salt Lake City.

**   1964   Appendix II: Survey and Tested Sites. *In* "1962 Excavations, Glen Canyon Area," Floyd W. Sharrock, et al. *University of Utah Anthropological Papers*, No. 73, *Glen Canyon Series*, No. 25, pp. 139–56. Salt Lake City.

**Day, Kent C.
  1966   Excavations at Gunlock Flats, Southwestern Utah. *University of Utah Anthropological Papers*, in preparation. Salt Lake City.

**Day, Kent C. and David S. Dibble
  1963   Archeological Survey of the Flaming Gorge Reservoir Area, Wyoming-Utah. *University of Utah Anthropological Papers*, No. 65, *Upper Colorado Series*, No. 9. Salt Lake City.

**Dean, Jeffrey S.
  1964   Summary of Tree-Ring Material from Southern Utah. Addendum *In* "1962 Excavations, Glen Canyon Area," Floyd W. Sharrock, et al. *University of Utah Anthropological Papers*, No. 73, *Glen Canyon Series*, No. 25, pp. 167–73. Salt Lake City.

**Dibble, David S. and Kent C. Day
  1962   A Preliminary Survey of the Fontenelle Reservoir, Wyoming. *University of Utah Anthropological Papers*, No. 58, *Upper Colorado Series*, No. 7. Salt Lake City.

Dittert, Alfred E., Jr., Frank W. Eddy and Beth L. Dickey
  1963   Evidences of Early Ceramic Phases in the Navajo Reservoir District. *E1 Palacio*, Vol. 70, Nos. 1–2, pp. 5–12. Santa Fe.

**Dotson, Phil
  1960   Appendix B: Notes on Diseases, Parasites, Food, and Condition of Green River Fishes, 1959. *In* "Ecological Studies of the Flora and Fauna of Flam-

ing Gorge Reservoir Basin, Utah and Wyoming," Seville Flowers, et al. *University of Utah Anthropological Papers*, No. 48, *Upper Colorado Series*, No. 3, pp. 169–75. Salt Lake City.

Durrant, Stephen D.
    1952   Mammals of Utah, Taxonomy and Distribution. *University of Kansas Publications, Museum of National History*, Vol. 6. Lawrence.

Eddy, Frank W. and Beth L. Dickey
    1961   Excavations at Los Pinos Phase Sites in the Navajo Reservoir District. *Museum of New Mexico Papers in Anthropology*, No. 4, *Navajo Project Studies*, No. 4. Santa Fe.

**Euler, Robert C.
    1964   Southern Paiute Archaeology. *American Antiquity*, Vol. 29, No. 3, pp. 379–81. Salt Lake City.

**   1966   Southern Paiute Ethnohistory. *University of Utah Anthropological Papers*, No. 78, *Glen Canyon Series*, No. 28. Salt Lake City.

Ferdon, Edwin N., Jr.
    1955   A Trial Survey of Mexican-Southwestern Architectural Parallels. *Monographs of the School of American Research*, No. 21. Santa Fe.

**Flowers, Seville
    1959   Appendix D: Algae Collected in Glen Canyon. *In* "Ecological Studies of the Flora and Fauna in Glen Canyon, Angus M. Woodbury, et al. *University of Utah Anthropological Papers*, No. 40, *Glen Canyon Series*, No. 7, pp. 203–5. Salt Lake City.

**Flowers, Seville, et al.
    1960   Ecological Studies of the Flora and Fauna of Flaming Gorge Reservoir Basin, Utah and Wyoming. *University of Utah Anthropological Papers*, No. 48, *Upper Colorado Series*, No. 3. Salt Lake City.

**Flowers, Seville, Heber H. Hall and Gerald T. Groves
    1960   Appendix: Annotated List of Plants Found in Flaming Gorge Reservoir Basin, 1959. *In* "Ecological Studies of the Flora and Fauna of Flaming Gorge Reservoir Basin, Utah and Wyoming," Seville Flowers, et al. *University of Utah Anthropological Papers*, No. 48, *Upper Colorado Series*, No. 3, pp. 49–98. Salt Lake City.

*Foster, Gene
    1952   A Brief Archaeological Survey of Glen Canyon. *Plateau*, Vol. 25, No. 2, pp. 21–26. Flagstaff.

*   1954   Petrographic Art in Glen Canyon. *Plateau*, Vol. 27, No. 1, pp. 6–18. Flagstaff.

**Fowler, Don D.
1958 Archeological Survey in Glen Canyon: A Preliminary Report of 1958 Work. *Utah Archaeology: A Newsletter*, Vol. 4, No. 4, pp. 14–16. Salt Lake City.

** 1959 Glen Canyon Main Stem Survey. In "The Glen Canyon Archeological Survey, Part II," Don D. Fowler, et al. *University of Utah Anthropological Papers*, No. 39, *Glen Canyon Series*, No. 6, pp. 473–540. Salt Lake City.

** 1961a Appendix II: Lake Canyon Survey. In "1960 Excavations, Glen Canyon Area," Floyd W. Sharrock, et al. *University of Utah Anthropological Papers*, No. 52, *Glen Canyon Series*, No. 14, pp. 286–337. Salt Lake City.

** 1961b 1960 Archaeological Survey and Testing in the Glen Canyon Region. *Utah Archaeology: A Newsletter*, Vol. 7, No. 1, pp. 18–24. Salt Lake City.

** 1963 1961 Excavations, Harris Wash, Utah. *University of Utah Anthropological Papers*, No. 64, *Glen Canyon Series*, No. 19. Salt Lake City.

**Fowler, Don D., et al.
1959 The Glen Canyon Archeological Survey, Parts, I, II and III. *University of Utah Anthropological Papers*, No. 39, *Glen Canyon Series*, No. 6. Salt Lake City.

**Fowler, Don D. and C. Melvin Aikens
1962 A Preliminary Report of 1961 Excavations in Harris Wash and on the Kaiparowits Plateau. *Utah Archaeology: A Newsletter*, Vol. 8, No. 1, pp. 5–13. Salt Lake City.

** 1963 1961 Excavations, Kaiparowits Plateau, Utah. *University of Utah Anthropological Papers*, No. 66, *Glen Canyon Series*, No. 20. Salt Lake City.

Fritts, Harold C.
1965 Tree-Ring Evidence for Climatic Changes in Western North America. *Monthly Weather Review*, Vol. 93, No. 7, pp. 421–43. Washington.

*Gaines, Xerpha M.
1957 Plants in Glen Canyon. *Plateau*, Vol. 30, No. 2, pp. 31–34. Flagstaff.

*Gaines, Xerpha M.
1960 An Annotated Catalogue of Glen Canyon Plants. *Museum of Northern Arizona Technical Series*, No. 4. Flagstaff.

Gillin, John
1941 Archeological Investigations in Central Utah. *Papers of the Peabody Museum of American Archeology and Ethnology*, Vol. 17, No. 2. Cambridge.

1955   Archeological Investigations in Nine Mile Canyon, Utah: A Re-Publication. *University of Utah Anthropological Papers*, No. 21. Salt Lake City.

Gladwin, Harold Sterling
       n.d.   Tree-Ring Analysis; Tree-Rings and Droughts. *Medallion Papers*, No. 37. Globe.

Glock, Waldo S.
       1937   Principles and Methods of Tree-Ring Analysis. *Carnegie Institution of Washington Publication*, No. 486. Washington.

**Gunnerson, James H.
       1958   Kaiparowits Plateau Archeological Survey, A Preliminary Report. *Utah Archaeology: A Newsletter*, Vol. 4, No. 3, pp. 9–20. Salt Lake City.

**   1959a Archeological Survey of the Kaiparowits Plateau. *In* "The Glen Canyon Archeological Survey, Part II," Don D. Fowler, et al. *University of Utah Anthropological Papers*, No. 39, *Glen Canyon Series*, No. 6, pp. 318–471. Salt Lake City.

**   1959b 1957 Excavations, Glen Canyon Area. *University of Utah Anthropological Papers*, No. 43, *Glen Canyon Series*, No. 10. Salt Lake City.

       1960   The Fremont Culture: Internal Dimensions and External Relationships. *American Antiquity*, Vol. 25, No. 3, pp. 373–80. Salt Lake City.

Hack, John T.
       1942   The Changing Physical Environment of the Hopi Indians of Arizona. *Papers of the Peabody Museum of American Archaeology and Ethnology*, Vol. 35, No. 1, *Awatovi Expedition Reports*, No. 1. Cambridge.

**Hargrave, Lyndon L.
       1960   Appendix II: Identification of Archeological Feathers from Glen Canyon, Utah. *In* "1958 Excavations, Glen Canyon Area," William D. Lipe. *University of Utah Anthropological Papers*, No. 44, *Glen Canyon Series*, No. 11, pp. 239–41. Salt Lake City.

**   1961   Appendix I: Bird Bones from the Coombs Site. *In* "The Coombs Site, Part II, Summary and Conclusions," Robert H. Lister and Florence C. Lister. *University of Utah Anthropological Papers*, No. 41, *Glen Canyon Series*, No. 8, pp. 114–16. Salt Lake City.

*Haring, Inez M.
       1961   Mosses of the Glen Canyon Area. *Plateau*, Vol. 33, No. 4, pp. 120–22. Flagstaff.

*Haskell, Horace S.
       1958   Flowering Plants in Glen Canyon—Late Summer Aspect. *Plateau*, Vol. 31, No. 1, pp. 1–3. Flagstaff.

Haury, Emil W.
    1956   Speculations on Prehistoric Settlement Patterns in the Southwest. *In* "Prehistoric Settlement Patterns in the New World," Gordon R. Willey (ed.). *Viking Fund Publications in Anthropology*, No. 23, pp. 3–10. New York.

    1958   Evidence at Point of Pines for a Prehistoric Migration from Northern Arizona. *Contribution to Point of Pines Archaeology*, No. 12. *In* "Migrations in New World Culture History," Raymond H. Thompson (ed.). *University of Arizona Bulletin*, Vol. 29, No. 2, *Social Science Bulletin*, No. 27, pp. 1–6. Tucson.

Herold, Joyce
    1961   Prehistoric Settlement and Physical Environment in the Mesa Verde Area. *University of Utah Anthropological Papers*, No. 58. Salt Lake City.

Hewes, Gordon W.
    1952   California Flicker–Quill Headbands in the Light of an Ancient Colorado Cave Specimen. *American Antiquity*, vol. 18, No. 2, pp. 147–54. Salt Lake City.

Hobler, Philip M.
    1965   *The Late Survival of Pithouse Architecture in the Kayenta Anasazi Area*. MA thesis, University of Arizona, Department of Anthropology. Tucson.

Hunt, Charles B.
    1955   Recent Geology of Cane Wash, Monument Valley, Arizona. *Science*, Vol. 122, No. 3170, pp. 583–85. Washington.

    1956   Cenozoic Geology of the Colorado Plateau. *U.S. Geological Survey Professional Paper*, No. 279. Washington.

Jennings, Jesse D.
    1955   *The Archeology of the Plains: An Assessment (with Special Reference to the Missouri River Basin)*. (Limited distribution.) National Park Service, memorandum of Agreement No. 14-10-0100-287 with University of Utah Anthropology Department. Salt Lake City.

    1956   The American Southwest: A Problem in Cultural Isolation. *In* "Seminars in Archaeology: 1955," Robert Wauchope (ed.). *American Antiquity*, Vol. 22, No. 2, Pt. 2, *Memoirs of the Society for American Archaeology*, No. 11, pp. 59–127. Salt Lake City.

    1957a   Danger Cave. *University of Utah Anthropological Papers*, No. 27. Salt Lake City. (Also released as *American Antiquity*, Vol. 23, No. 2, Pt. 2, *Memoirs of the Society for American Archaeology*, No. 14. Salt Lake City.)

**   1957b   Upper Colorado River Basin Archeological Salvage Project: Summer 1957. *Utah Archaeology: A Newsletter*, Vol. 3, No. 3, pp. 7–9. Salt Lake City.

**   1959a Appendix A: Operational Manual: University of Utah–National Park Service Upper Colorado River Basin Archeological Salvage Project. *In* "The Glen Canyon Archeological Survey, Part II," Don D. Fowler, et al. *University of Utah Anthropological Papers*, No. 39, *Glen Canyon Series*, No. 6, pp. 677–707. Salt Lake City.

**   1959b Introductory History. *In* "The Glen Canyon Archeological Survey, Part I," Don D. Fowler, et al. *University of Utah Anthropological Papers*, No. 39, *Glen Canyon Series*, No. 6, pp. 1–13. Salt Lake City.

**   1960 Early Man in Utah. *Utah Historical Quarterly*, Vol. 28, No. 1, pp. 3–27. Salt Lake City.

**   1961 Salvage and Scholarship. *Northwestern University Tri-Quarterly*, Vol. 3, No. 2, pp. 43–47. Evanston.

**   1963a Administration of Contract Emergency Archaeological Programs. *American Antiquity*, Vol. 28, No. 3, pp. 282–85. Salt Lake City.

**   1963b Anthropology and the World of Science. Twenty-seventh Annual Frederick William Reynolds Lecture. *University of Utah Bulletin*, Vol. 54, No. 18. Salt Lake City.

         1965 Perspective. *In The Native Americans*, Robert F. Spencer and Jess D. Jennings (eds.), pp. 7–56. Harper and Row, New York.

**   1966 Glen Canyon: A Summary. *University of Utah Anthropological Papers*, No. 81, *Glen Canyon Series*, No. 31. Salt Lake City.

**Jennings, Jesse D. and Floyd W. Sharrock
         1965 The Glen Canyon: A Multi-Discipline Project. *Utah Historical Quarterly*, Vol. 33, No. 1, pp. 35–50. Salt Lake City.

**Kelly, Isabel T.
         1964 Southern Paiute Ethnology. *University of Utah Anthropological Papers*, No. 69, *Glen Canyon Series*, No. 21. Salt Lake City.

**Lance, John F.
         1963 Appendix IV: Alluvial Stratigraphy in Lake and Moqui Canyons. *In* "1961 Excavations, Glen Canyon Area," Floyd W. Sharrock, Kent C. Day and David S. Dibble. *University of Utah Anthropological Papers*, No. 63, *Glen Canyon Series*, No. 18, pp. 347–76. Salt Lake City.

Lehmer, Donald J.
         1954a Archeological Investigations in the Oahe Dam Area, South Dakota, 1950–51. *Bureau of American Ethnology Bulletin*, No. 158, *River Basin Survey Papers*, No. 7. Washington.

1954b The Sedentary Horizon of the Northern Plains. *Southwestern Journal of Anthropology*, Vol. 10, No. 2, pp. 139–59. Albuquerque.

*Lindsay, Alexander J., Jr.
1961a The Beaver Creek Agricultural Community on the San Juan River, Utah. *American Antiquity*, Vol. 27, No. 2, pp. 174–87. Salt Lake City.

*   1961B Saving Prehistoric Sites in the Southwest. *Archaeology*, Vol. 14, No. 4, pp. 245–49. Columbia.

*Lindsay, Alexander J., Jr., et al.
1965 *Survey and Excavations North and East of Navajo Mountain, Utah, 1960–61.* Unpublished Ms., Museum of Northern Arizona. Flagstaff.

*Lindsay, Alexander J., Jr., and J. Richard Ambler
1963 Recent Contributions and Research Problems in Kayenta Anasazi Prehistory. *Plateau*, Vol. 35, No. 3, pp. 86–92. Flagstaff.

*Lindsay, Alexander J., Jr., Christy G. Turner II and Paul V. Long, Jr.
1962 *Archaeological Excavations Along the Lower San Juan River, Utah, 1958–1960.* Unpublished Ms., Museum of Northern Arizona. Flagstaff.

**Lindsay, Delbert S.
1959 Appendix A: Vascular Plants Collected in Glen Canyon. *In* "Ecological Studies of the Flora and Fauna in Glen Canyon," Angus M. Woodbury, et al., *University of Utah Anthropological Papers*, No. 40, *Glen Canyon Series*, No. 7, pp. 63–72. Salt Lake City.

**Lipe, William D.
1958 Archeological Excavations in Glen Canyon: A Preliminary Report of 1958 Work. *Utah Archaeology: A Newsletter*, Vol. 4, No. 4, pp. 4–13. Salt Lake City.

**   1960 1958 Excavations, Glen Canyon Area. *University of Utah Anthropological Papers*, No. 44, *Glen Canyon Series*, No. 11. Salt Lake City.

**Lipe, William D., et al.
1960 1959 Excavations, Glen Canyon Area. *University of Utah Anthropological Papers*, No. 49, *Glen Canyon Series*, No. 13. Salt Lake City.

**Lister, Florence C.
1964 Kaiparowits Plateau and Glen Canyon Prehistory: An Interpretation Based on Ceramics. *University of Utah Anthropological Papers*, No. 71, *Glen Canyon Series*, No. 23. Salt Lake City.

**Lister, Robert H.
1958a The Glen Canyon Survey in 1957. *University of Utah Anthropological Papers, Glen Canyon Series*, No. 1. Salt Lake City.

**   1958b A Preliminary Note on Excavations at the Coombs Site, Boulder, Utah. *Utah Archaeology: A Newsletter*, Vol. 4, No. 3, pp. 4–8. Salt Lake City.

**   1959a The Glen Canyon Right Bank Survey. *In* "The Glen Canyon Archeological Survey, Part I," Don D. Fowler, et al. *University of Utah Anthropological Papers*, No. 39, *Glen Canyon Series*, No. 6, pp. 27–162. Salt Lake City.

**   1959b The Waterpocket Fold: A Distributional Problem. *In* "The Glen Canyon Archeological Survey, Part I," Don D. Fowler, et al. *University of Utah Anthropological Papers*, No. 39, *Glen Canyon Series*, No. 6, pp. 285–317. Salt Lake City.

**   1960 *Site Testing Program, 1960, San Juan Triangle Area and Escalante, Utah.* (Dittoed, limited distribution.) University of Utah, Anthropology Department. Salt Lake City.

**Lister, Robert H., J. Richard Ambler and Florence C. Lister
        1959–1961 The Coombs Site, Parts I, II and III. *University of Utah Anthropological Papers*, No. 41, *Glen Canyon Series*, No. 8. Salt Lake City.

*Long, Paul V., Jr.
        1965 *Archaeological Excavations in Glen Canyon, Utah-Arizona, 1959–1960.* MA thesis, University of Arizona, Department of Anthropology, Tucson. (Also published 1966 *Museum of Northern Arizona Bulletin*, No. 42, *Glen Canyon Series*, No. 7. Flagstaff.)

*Long, Paul V., Jr., Christy G. Turner II and Alexander J. Lindsay, Jr.
        1963 Excavations in Lower Glen Canyon, Utah, 1959–1960. *Museum of Northern Arizona Bulletin*, No. 40, *Glen Canyon Series*, No. 6. Flagstaff.

Macneish, R. S.
        1964 Ancient Mesoamerican Civilization. *Science*, Vol. 143, No. 3606, pp. 531–537. Washington.

**Martin, Paul S.
        1964 Pollen Analysis in the Glen Canyon. Addendum *In* "1962 Excavations, Glen Canyon Area," Floyd W. Sharrock, et al. *University of Utah Anthropological Papers*, No. 73, *Glen Canyon Series*, No. 25, pp. 176–95. Salt Lake City.

Martin, Paul S., et al.
        1952 Mogollon Cultural Continuity and Change. *Fieldiana: Anthropology*, Vol. 40. Chicago.

        1962 Chapters in the Prehistory of Eastern Arizona, I. *Fieldiana: Anthropology*, Vol. 53. Chicago.

**Martin, Paul S. and Floyd W. Sharrock
1964   Pollen Analysis of Prehistoric Human Feces: A New Approach to Ethnobotany. *American Antiquity*, Vol. 30, No. 2, pp. 168–80. Salt Lake City. (Also published as *University of Arizona Contribution*, No. 86, *Program in Geochronology*. Tucson.)

**McDonald, Donald B.
1959   Appendix C: Fish Stomach Contents. *In* "Ecological Studies of the Flora and Fauna in Glen Canyon," Angus M. Woodbury, et al. *University of Utah Anthropological Papers*, No. 40, *Glen Canyon Series*, No. 7, pp. 201–2. Salt Lake City.

*McDougall, Walter B.
1959   *Plants of the Glen Canyon Area in the Herbarium of the Museum of Northern Arizona*. Mimeographed, Museum of Northern Arizona. Flagstaff.

McGregor, John C.
1965   *Southwestern Archaeology*. 2nd ed. University of Illinois Press. Urbana.

Meighan, Clement W., et al.
1956   Archeological Excavations in Iron County, Utah. *University of Utah Anthropological Papers*, No. 25. Salt Lake City.

Miller, David E.
1958   Discovery of Glen Canyon, 1776. *Utah Historical Quarterly*, Vol. 26, No. 3, pp. 220–37. Salt Lake City.

1959   *Hole-In-The-Rock; an Epic in the Colonization of the Great American West*. University of Utah Press. Salt Lake City.

*Miller, William C. and David A. Breternitz
1958a   1957 Navajo Canyon Survey—Preliminary Report. *Plateau*, Vol. 30, No. 3, pp. 72–74. Flagstaff.

1958b   1958 Navajo Canyon Survey—Preliminary Report. *Plateau*, Vol. 31, No. 1, pp. 3–7. Flagstaff.

Mullens, Thomas E.
1960   Geology of the Clay Hills Area, San Juan County, Utah. *U.S. Geological Survey Bulletin*, No. 1087-H. Washington, D.C.

*Musser, Guy G.
1959   Appendix E: Annotated Check List of Aquatic Inspects of Glen Canyon. *In* "Ecological Studies of the Flora and Fauna in Glen Canyon," Angus M. Woodbury, et al. *University of Utah Anthropological Papers*, No. 40, *Glen Canyon Series*, No. 7, pp. 207–21. Salt Lake City.

Nusbaum, Jesse Logan
    1922   A Basket-Maker Cave in Kane County, Utah. *Indian Notes and Monographs, Miscellaneous*, No. 29. New York.

Osborne, Douglas, et al.
    1965   Contributions of the Wetherill Mesa Archeological Project. *American Antiquity*, Vol. 31, No. 2, Pt. 2, *Memoirs of the Society for American Archaeology*, No. 19. Salt Lake City.

Osborne, Douglas, Alan Bryan and Robert H. Crabtree
    1961   The Sheep Island Site and the Mid-Columbia Valley. *River Basin Survey Paper*, No. 24. *In Bureau of American Ethnology Bulletin*, No. 179, pp. 267–306. Washington.

**Pendergast, David M.
    1961a   1960 Test Excavations in the Plainfield Reservoir Area. Addendum *In* "1960 Excavations, Glen Canyon Area," Floyd W. Sharrock, et al., *University of Utah Anthropological Papers*, No. 52, *Glen Canyon Series*, No. 14. 12 pp. Salt Lake City.

**   1961b   USAS–UCRBASP Joint Excavation in the Plainfield Reservoir. *Utah Archaeology: A Newsletter*, Vol. 7, No. 3, pp. 15–21. Salt Lake City.

**   1963   Lithic Materials from Southwestern Wyoming and Northeastern Utah. Addendum *In* "Archeological Survey of the Flaming Gorge Reservoir Area, Wyoming-Utah," Kent C. Day and David S. Dibble. *University of Utah Anthropological Papers*, No. 65, *Upper Colorado Series*, No. 9. 16 pp. Salt Lake City.

Phillips, Philip, James A. Ford, and James B. Griffin
    1951   Archaeological Survey in the Lower Mississippi Alluvial Valley, 1940–1947. *Papers of the Peabody Museum of American Archaeology and Ethnology*, Vol. 25. Cambridge.

**Purdy, William M.
    1959a   Appendix I: Final Report; Preliminary Survey of the Flaming Gorge Reservoir, 1958. *In* "An Outline of the History of the Flaming Gorge Area," William M. Purdy. *University of Utah Anthropological Papers*, No. 37, *Upper Colorado Series*, No. 1, pp. 37–39. Salt Lake City.

**   1959b   An Outline of the History of the Flaming Gorge Area. *University of Utah Anthropological Papers*, No. 37, *Upper Colorado Series*, No. 1. Salt Lake City.

Raisz, Erwin
    1946   *Map of the Landforms of the United States*. 4th rev. ed. To accompany Atwood's *Physiographic Provinces of North America*. Prepared at the Institute of Geographical Exploration, Harvard University. Cambridge.

**Reed, Erik K.

 1963a Appendix III: Human Skeletal Material from Moqui Canyon, Southeastern Utah. *In* "1961 Excavations, Glen Canyon Area," Floyd W. Sharrock, Kent C. Day and David S. Dibble. *University of Utah Anthropological Papers*, No. 63, *Glen Canyon Series*, No. 18, pp. 307–46. Salt Lake City.

 1963b The Period Known as Pueblo I. *Regional Research Abstract*, No. 304. National Park Service. Santa Fe.

** 1964a Appendix III: Human Skeletal Material, 1962 Excavations, Glen Canyon Area. *In* "1962 Excavations, Glen Canyon Area," Floyd W. Sharrock, et al. *University of Utah Anthropological Papers*, No. 73, *Glen Canyon Series*, No. 25, pp. 157–63. Salt Lake City.

 1964b The Greater Southwest. *In Prehistoric Man in the New World*, Jesse D. Jennings and Edward Norbeck (eds.), pp. 175–92. Rice University Semicentennial Publications, University of Chicago Press. Chicago.

Ridd, Merrill K.

 1963 Landforms of Utah in Proportional Relief. *Map Supplement*, No. 3. *In Annals of the Association of American Cartographers*, Vol. 53, No. 4. Washington.

Roberts, Frank H. H., Jr.

 1935 A Survey of Southwestern Archaeology. *American Anthropologist*, Vol. 37, No. 1, pp. 1–35. Menasha.

 1937 Archaeology in the Southwest. *American Antiquity*, Vol. 3, No. 1, pp. 3–33. Salt Lake City.

Rohn, Arthur H.

 1963 Prehistoric Soil and Water Conservation on Chapin Mesa, Southwestern Colorado. *American Antiquity*, Vol. 28, No. 4, pp. 441–55. Salt Lake City.

Sayles, E. B. and Ernst Antevs

 1941 The Cochise Culture. *Medallion Papers*, No. 9. Globe.

Schoenwetter, James

 1962 The Pollen Analysis of Eighteen Archeological Sites in Arizona and New Mexico. *In* "Chapters in the Prehistory of Eastern Arizona, I," Paul S. Martin, *et al. Fieldiana: Anthropology*, Vol. 53, pp. 168–209. Chicago.

Schoenwetter, James, Frank W. Eddy and Eleanor Jane Nettle

 1964 Alluvial and Palynological Reconstruction of Environments, Navajo Reservoir District. *Museum of New Mexico Papers in Anthropology*, No. 13, Navajo Project Studies, No. 11. Santa Fe.

Schroeder, Albert H.
1955 Archeology of Zion Park. *University of Utah Anthropological Papers*, No. 22. Salt Lake City.

1965 Unregulated Diffusion from Mexico into the Southwest Prior to A.D. 700. *American Antiquity*, Vol. 30, No. 3, pp. 297–309. Salt Lake City.

Schulman, Edmund
1948 Dendrochronology in Northeastern Utah. *Tree-Ring Bulletin*, Vol. 15, Nos. 1/2, pp. 1–14. Tucson.

1956 *Dendroclimatic Changes in Semiarid America*. University of Arizona Press. Tucson.

**Sharrock, Floyd W.
1961a A Preliminary Report of 1960 Archeological Excavations in Glen Canyon. *Utah Archaeology: A Newsletter*, Vol. 7, No. 1, pp. 7–15. Salt Lake City.

** 1961b A Preliminary Report of 1961 Archeological Excavations in Moqui Canyon and Castle Wash. *Utah Archaeology: A Newsletter*, Vol. 7, No. 4, pp. 6–11. Salt Lake City.

** 1961c University of Utah 1961 Field Season. *Utah Archaeology: A Newsletter*, Vol. 7, No. 1, p. 24. Salt Lake City.

** 1961d University of Utah 1962 Field Season. *Utah Archaeology: A Newsletter*, Vol. 7, No. 4, p. 15. Salt Lake City.

** 1963a The Hazzard Collection. *Archives of Archaeology*, No. 23. Society for American Archaeology and the University of Wisconsin Press. Madison.

** 1963b A Preliminary Report of 1962 Archeological Excavations in Glen Canyon. *Utah Archaeology: A Newsletter*, Vol. 8, No. 4, pp. 1–3. Salt Lake City.

1966a *Archeological Survey of Canyonlands National Park*. Unpublished Ms. On file, University of Utah, Anthropology Department. Salt Lake City.

1966b *Prehistoric Occupational Patterns in Southwest Wyoming and Cultural Relationships with the Great Basin and Plains Culture Areas*. Ph.D. dissertation, University of Utah, Anthropology Department, Salt Lake City (Also published as *University of Utah Anthropological Papers*, No. 77. Salt Lake City). (Work was an outgrowth of UCRBASP.)

**Sharrock, Floyd W., et al.
1961b 1960 Excavations, Glen Canyon Area. *University of Utah Anthropological Papers* No. 52, *Glen Canyon Series*, No. 14. Salt Lake City.

** 1964 1962 Excavations, Glen Canyon Area. *University of Utah Anthropological Papers*, No. 73, *Glen Canyon Series*, No. 25. Salt Lake City.

**Sharrock, Floyd W., Kent C. Day and David S. Dibble
1963 1961 Excavations, Glen Canyon Area. *University of Utah Anthropological Papers*, No. 63, *Glen Canyon Series*, No. 18. Salt Lake City.

**Sharrock, Floyd W., David S. Dibble and Keith M. Anderson
1961a The Creeping Dune Irrigation Site in Glen Canyon, Utah. *American Antiquity*, Vol. 27, No. 2, pp. 188–202. Salt Lake City.

**Sharrock, Floyd W. and Edward G. Keane
1962 Carnegie Museum Collection for Southeast Utah. *University of Utah Anthropological Papers*, No. 57, *Glen Canyon Series*, No. 16. Salt Lake City.

Shiner, Joel L.
1961 The McNary Reservoir: A Study in Plateau Archeology. *River Basin Survey Paper*, No. 23. *In Bureau of American Ethnology Bulletin*, No. 179, pp. 149–266. Washington.

Shutler, Richard, Jr.
1961 Lost City; Pueblo Grande de Nevada. *Nevada State Museum Anthropological Papers*, No. 5. Carson City.

Shutler, Richard, Jr., and Mary Elizabeth Shutler
1962 Archeological Survey in Southern Nevada. *Nevada State Museum Anthropological Papers*, No. 7. Carson City.

**Smith, Gerald R.
1959a Appendix A: Annotated List of Fishes of the Flaming Gorge Reservoir Basin, 1959. *In* "Ecological Studies of the Flora and Fauna of Flaming Gorge Reservoir Basin, Utah and Wyoming," Seville Flowers, *et al. University of Utah Anthropological Papers*, No. 48, *Upper Colorado Series*, No. 3, pp. 163–68. Salt Lake City.

** 1959b Appendix B: Annotated Check List of Fishes of Glen Canyon. *In* "Ecological Studies of the Flora and Fauna in Glen Canyon." Angus M. Woodbury, *et al. University of Utah Anthropological Papers*, No. 40, *Glen Canyon Series*, No. 7, pp. 195–99. Salt Lake City.

**Smith, Gerald R., Guy Musser and Donald B. McDonald
1959 Appendix A: Aquatic Survey Tabulation. *In* "Ecological Studies of the Flora and Fauna in Glen Canyon," Angus M. Woodbury, *et al. University of Utah Anthropological Papers*, No. 40, *Glen Canyon Series*, No. 7, pp. 177–94. Salt Lake City.

**Smith, Ted C.
1965   Linwood, Utah: Socio-historical Study. *University of Utah Anthropological Papers*, in preparation. Salt Lake City.

Steward, Julian H.
1933a   Archaeological Problems of the Northern Periphery of the Southwest. *Museum of Northern Arizona Bulletin*, No. 5. Flagstaff.

1933b   Early Inhabitants of Western Utah, Part I. Mounds and House Types. *University of Utah Bulletin*, Vol. 23, No. 7, pp. 1–34. Salt Lake City.

1936   Pueblo Material Culture in Western Utah. *University of New Mexico Bulletin*, Whole No. 287, *Anthropological Series*, Vol. 1, No. 3. Albuquerque.

1940   Native Cultures of the Intermontane (Great Basin) Area. *In* "Essays in Historical Anthropology of North America." *Smithsonian Miscellaneous Collections*, Vol. 100, pp. 445–502. Washington.

1941   Archeological Reconnaissance of Southern Utah. *Bureau of American Ethnology Bulletin*, No. 128, *Anthropological Papers*, No. 18. Washington.

Stewart, Guy R.
1940   Conservation in Pueblo Agriculture: I, Primitive Practices; II, Present-day Flood Water Irrigation. *Scientific Monthly*, Vol. 51, Nos. 3–4, pp. 201–20. New York.

Stewart, Omer C.
1956   Fire as the First Great Force Employed by Man. *In Man's Role in Changing the Face of the Earth*, William L. Thomas, Jr. (ed.), pp. 115–33. University of Chicago Press, Chicago.

**Suhm, Dee Ann
1959a   Extended Survey of the Right Bank of the Glen Canyon. *In* "The Glen Canyon Archeological Survey, Part I," Don D. Fowler, *et al. University of Utah Anthropological Papers*, No. 39, *Glen Canyon Series*, No. 6, pp. 163–284. Salt Lake City.

**   1959b   *A Report on Investigations at Two Archeological Sites in the Flaming Gorge Reservoir Area, Daggett County, Utah*. Ms. On file, University of Utah, Anthropology Department. Salt Lake City.

**Suhm, Dee Ann
1960a   Additional Artifacts from the 1957 Excavations in the Glen Canyon. Addendum *In* "1959 Excavations, Glen Canyon Area," William D. Lipe, *et al. University of Utah Anthropological Papers*, No. 49, *Glen Canyon Series*, No. 13. 19 pp. Salt Lake City.

** 1960b Cataloguing Archeological Collections. *Utah Archaeology: A Newsletter*, Vol. 6, No. 2, pp. 5–10. Salt Lake City.

Swanton, John R.
1928 Aboriginal Culture of the Southeast. *Bureau of American Ethnology*, 42nd Annual Report, pp. 673–726. Washington.

**Sweeney, Catherine L.
1961 Ethnohistoric Study in the Glen Canyon. *Utah Archaeology: A Newsletter*, Vol. 9, No. 3, pp. 9–13. Salt Lake City.

**Sweeney, Catherine L., and Robert C. Euler
1963 Southern Paiute Archaeology in the Glen Canyon Drainage: A Preliminary Report. *Nevada State Museum Anthropological Papers*, No. 9. Carson City.

Taylor, Dee C.
1957 Two Fremont Sites and Their Position in Southwestern Prehistory. *University of Utah Anthropological Papers*, No. 29. Salt Lake City.

Taylor, Walter W.
1948 A Study of Archaeology. *American Anthropological Association Memoir*, No. 69. Menasha

*Turner, Christy G., II
1960a Appendix I: Infant Burials from the Catfish Canyon Site. *In* "1958 Excavations, Glen Canyon Area," William D. Lipe. *University of Utah Anthropological Papers*, No. 44, *Glen Canyon Series*, No. 11, pp. 233–38. Salt Lake City.

* 1960b Appendix II: Husteds Well Skeleton. *In.* "1959 Excavations, Glen Canyon Area," William D., Lipe, *et al. University of Utah Anthropological Papers*, No. 49, *Glen Canyon Series*, No. 13, pp. 237–38. Salt Lake City.

* 1960c The Location of Human Skeletons Excavated from Prehistoric Sites in the Southwestern United States. *Museum of Northern Arizona Technical Series*, No. 3. Flagstaff.

* 1960d Mystery Canyon Survey: San Juan County, Utah, 1959. *Plateau*, Vol. 32, No. 4, pp. 73–80. Flagstaff.

* 1961a Appendix II: Human Skeletons from the Coombs Site: Skeletal and Dental Aspects. *In* "The Coombs Site, Part III, Summary and Conclusions," Robert H. Lister and Florence C. Lister. *University of Utah Anthropological Papers*, No. 41, *Glen Canyon Series*, No. 8, pp. 117–36. Salt Lake City.

* 1961b Appendix III: Human Skeletal Material. *In* "1960 Excavations, Glen Canyon Area," Floyd W. Sharrock, *et al. University of Utah Anthropological Papers*, No. 52, *Glen Canyon Series*, No. 14, pp. 338–60. Salt Lake City.

*   1962a Further Baldrock Crescent Explorations, San Juan County, Utah, 1960. *Plateau*, Vol. 34, No. 4, pp. 101–12. Flagstaff.

*   1962b A Summary of the Archaeological Explorations of Dr. Byron Cummings in the Anasazi Culture Area. *Museum of Northern Arizona Technical Series*, No. 5. Flagstaff.

*   1963 Petrographs of the Glen Canyon Region: The Styles, Chronology, Distribution, and Relationships form Basketmaker to Navajo. *Museum of Northern Arizona Bulletin*, No. 38, *Glen Canyon Series*, No. 4. Flagstaff.

*Turner, Christy G., II, and Maurice E. Cooley
         1960 Prehistoric Use of Stone from the Glen Canyon Region. *Plateau*, Vol. 33, No. 2, pp. 46–53. Flagstaff.

*Turner, Christy G., II, and William C. Miller
         1961 1960 Northeast Navajo Mountain Survey. *Plateau*, Vol. 33, No. 3, pp. 57–68. Flagstaff.

Wasley, William W.
         1961 Techniques and Tools of Salvage. *Archaeology*, Vol. 14, No. 4, pp. 283–66. New York.

Wedel, Waldo R.
         1961 *Prehistoric Man on the Great Plains*. University of Oklahoma Press. Norman.

**Weller, Ted
         1959 San Juan Triangle Survey. *In* "The Glen Canyon Archeological Survey, Part II," Don D. Fowler, *et al. University of Utah Anthropological Papers*, No. 39, *Glen Canyon Series*, No. 6, pp. 543–675. Salt Lake City.

Wendorf, Fred
         1956 Some Distributions of Settlement Patterns in the Pueblo Southwest. *In* "Prehistoric Settlement Patterns in the New World," Gordon R. Willey (ed.). *Viking Fund Publications in Anthropology*, No. 23, pp. 18–25. New York.

         1962 *A Guide for Salvage Archaeology*. Museum of New Mexico. Santa Fe.

Willey, Gordon R. and Philip Phillips
         1958 *Method and Theory in American Archaeology*. The University of Chicago Press. Chicago.

Wood, W. Raymond
         1961 The Pomme de Terre Reservoir in Western Missouri. *The Missouri Archaeologist*, Vol. 23, pp. 1–131. Columbia.

**Woodbury, Angus
   1965   Notes on the Human Ecology of Glen Canyon. *University of Utah Anthropological Papers*, No. 74, *Glen Canyon Series*, No. 26. Salt Lake City.

**Woodbury, Angus M. and staff
   1957   *Working Plan for Ecological Studies*. U.S. National Park Service and the University of Utah Special Publication. Multilithed copy on file, University of Utah, Anthropology Department. Salt Lake City.

**Woodbury, Angus M., *et al.*
   1958   Preliminary Report on Biological Resources of the Glen Canyon Reservoir. *University of Utah Anthropological Papers*, No. 31, *Glen Canyon Series*, No. 2. Salt Lake City.

**   1959a Ecological Studies of Flora and Fauna in Glen Canyon. *University of Utah Anthropological Papers*, No. 40, *Glen Canyon Series*, No. 7. Salt Lake City.

**   1961   Ecological Studies of the Flora and Fauna of Navajo Reservoir Basin, Colorado and New Mexico. *University of Utah Anthropological Papers*, No. 55, *Upper Colorado Series*, No. 5. Salt Lake City.

**   1962   Ecological Studies of the Flora and Fauna of the Curecanti Reservoir Basins, Western Colorado. *University of Utah Anthropological Papers*, No. 59, *Upper Colorado Series*, No. 8. Salt Lake City.

**Woodbury, Angus M., Stephen D. Durrant and Seville Flowers
   1959b A Survey of Vegetation in Glen Canyon Reservoir Basin. *University of Utah Anthropological Papers*, No. 36, *Glen Canyon Series*, No. 5. Salt Lake City.

**   1960   A Survey of Vegetation in the Flaming Gorge Reservoir Basin. *University of Utah Anthropological Papers*, No. 45, *Upper Colorado Series*, No. 2. Salt Lake City.

**   1961   Survey of Vegetation in the Navajo Reservoir Basin. *University of Utah Anthropological Papers*, No. 51, *Upper Colorado Series*, No. 4. Salt Lake City.

**   1962   A Survey of Vegetation in the Curecanti Reservoir Basins. *University of Utah Anthropological Papers*, No. 56, *Upper Colorado Series*, No. 6. Salt Lake City.

Woodbury, Richard B.
   1954   Prehistoric Stone Implements of Northeastern Arizona. *Papers of the Peabody Museum of American Archaeology and Ethnology*, Vol. 34, *Reports of the Awatovi Expedition*, No. 6, Cambridge.

1961   Prehistoric Agriculture at Point of Pines, Arizona. *American Antiquity*, Vol. 26, No. 3, Pt. 2, *Memoirs of the Society for American Archaeology*, No. 17. Salt Lake City.

Wormington, Hannah M. and Robert H. Lister
1956   Archaeological Investigations on the Uncompahgre Plateau in West Central Colorado. *Denver Museum of Natural History Proceedings*, No. 2. Denver.

Yarnell, Richard A.
1965   Implications of Distinctive Flora on Pueblo Ruins. *American Anthropologist*, Vol. 67, No. 3, pp. 662–74. Menasha.

Zumberge, James H.
1963   *Elements of Geology*. Wiley and Sons. New York.